Disney

The Suite Life of Zack & Cody™

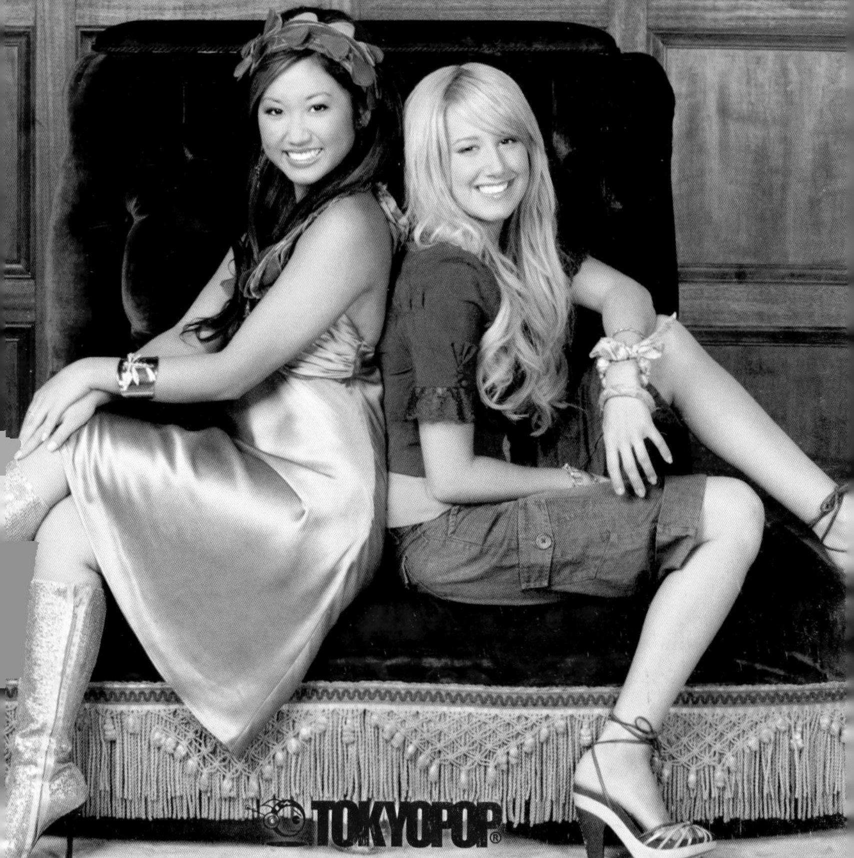

TOKYOPOP®

HAMBURG • LONDON • LOS ANGELES • TOKYO

Editor - Julie Taylor
Contributing Editor - Marion Brown
Cover and Graphic Designer - Monalisa J. de Asis
Graphic Artists - Lindsay Seligman and John Lo

Production Manager - Elisabeth Brizzi
Art Director - Anne Marie Horne
VP of Production - Ron Klamert
Editor in Chief - Rob Tokar
Publisher - Mike Kiley
President & C.O.O. - John Parker
C.E.O. & Chief Creative Officer - Stuart Levy

E-mail: info@TOKYOPOP.com
Come visit us online at www.TOKYOPOP.com

A TOKYOPOP® Cine-Manga® Book
TOKYOPOP Inc.
5900 Wilshire Blvd., Suite 2000
Los Angeles, CA 90036

The Suite Life of Zack and Cody
© 2007 Disney

ISBN: 978-1-4278-0752-6

First TOKYOPOP® printing: November 2007

10 9 8 7 6 5 4 3 2 1

Printed in the USA

DISNEY

The Suite Life
of Zack & Cody™

BASED ON THE TELEVISION SERIES,
"THE SUITE LIFE OF ZACK & CODY,"
CREATED BY DANNY KALLIS & JIM GEOGHAN

CONTENTS:

WHO'S WHO

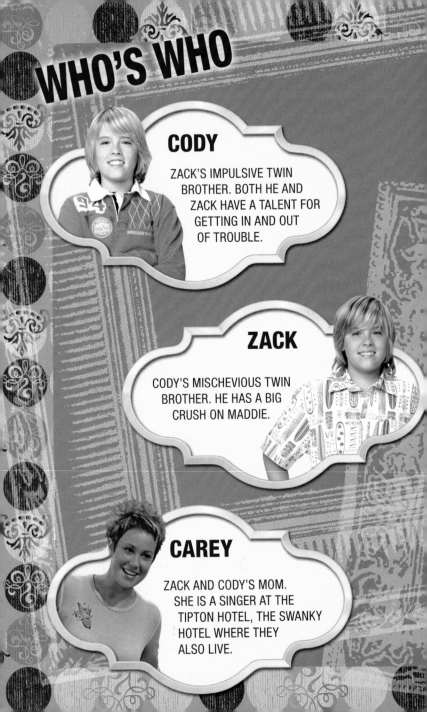

CODY

ZACK'S IMPULSIVE TWIN BROTHER. BOTH HE AND ZACK HAVE A TALENT FOR GETTING IN AND OUT OF TROUBLE.

ZACK

CODY'S MISCHEVIOUS TWIN BROTHER. HE HAS A BIG CRUSH ON MADDIE.

CAREY

ZACK AND CODY'S MOM. SHE IS A SINGER AT THE TIPTON HOTEL, THE SWANKY HOTEL WHERE THEY ALSO LIVE.

MADDIE

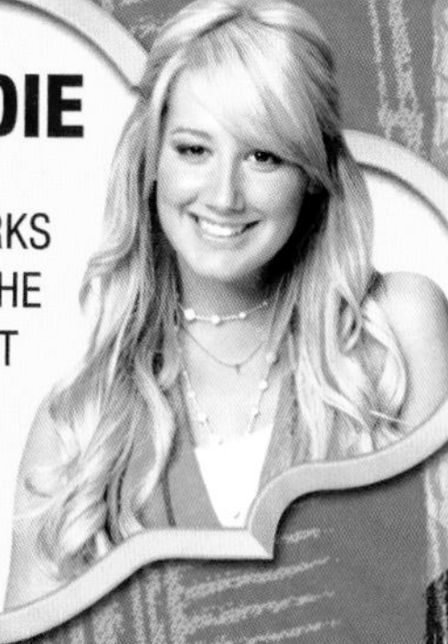

A SWEET GIRL WHO WORKS AT THE TIPTON HOTEL. SHE OFTEN HELPS THE TWINS OUT OF STICKY SITUATIONS.

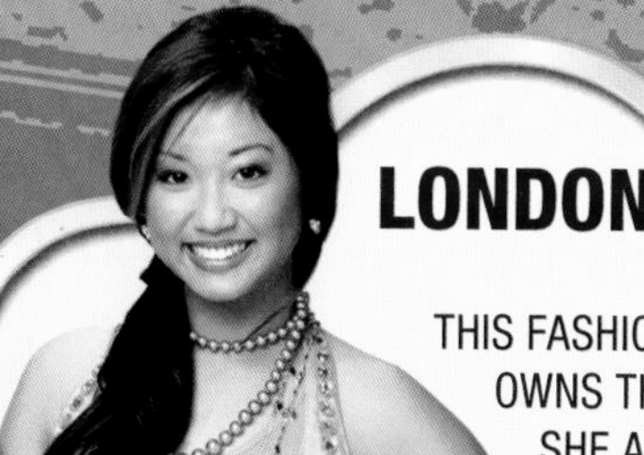

LONDON

THIS FASHIONISTA'S DAD OWNS THE TIPTON HOTEL. SHE AND MADDIE ARE RIVALS.

MR. MOSEBY

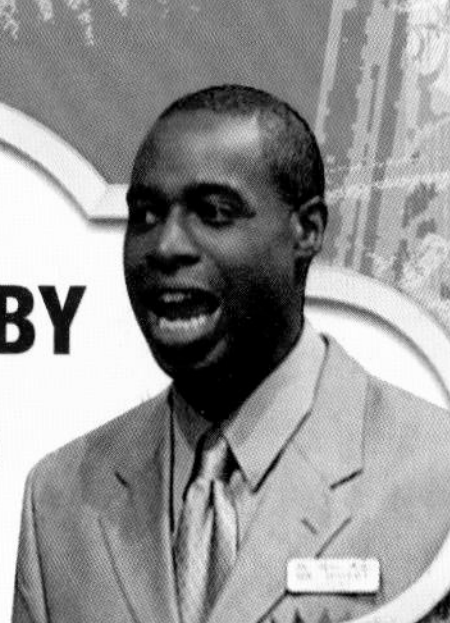

THE MEDDLING HOTEL MANAGER OF THE TIPTON HOTEL. HE OFTEN OBJECTS TO THE TWINS' ANTICS.

DISNEP

The Suite Life
of Zack & Cody

HOTEL HANGOUT

BASED ON THE EPISODE
WRITTEN BY JENY QUINE

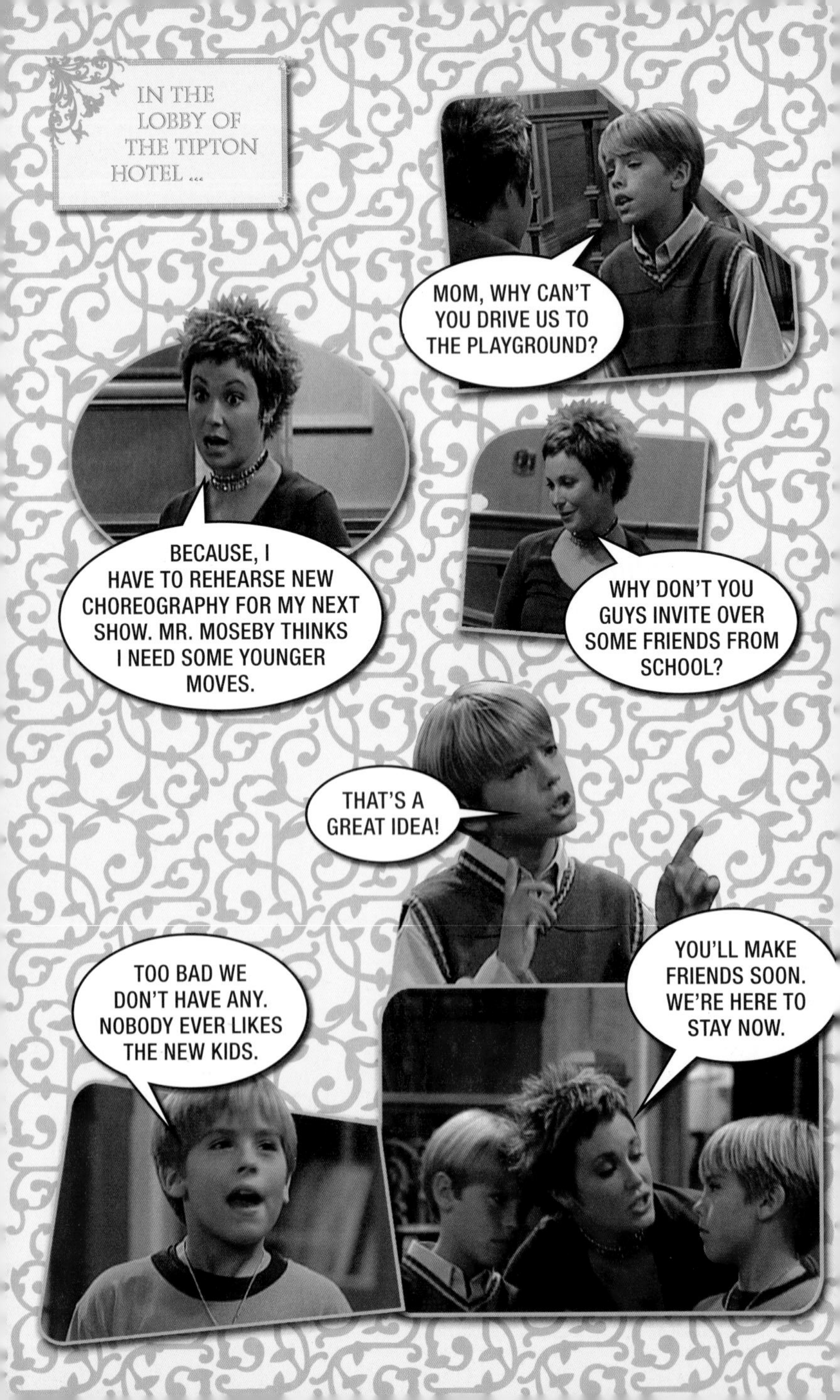
IN THE LOBBY OF THE TIPTON HOTEL ...
MOM, WHY CAN'T YOU DRIVE US TO THE PLAYGROUND?
BECAUSE, I HAVE TO REHEARSE NEW CHOREOGRAPHY FOR MY NEXT SHOW. MR. MOSEBY THINKS I NEED SOME YOUNGER MOVES.
WHY DON'T YOU GUYS INVITE OVER SOME FRIENDS FROM SCHOOL?
THAT'S A GREAT IDEA!
TOO BAD WE DON'T HAVE ANY. NOBODY EVER LIKES THE NEW KIDS.
YOU'LL MAKE FRIENDS SOON. WE'RE HERE TO STAY NOW.

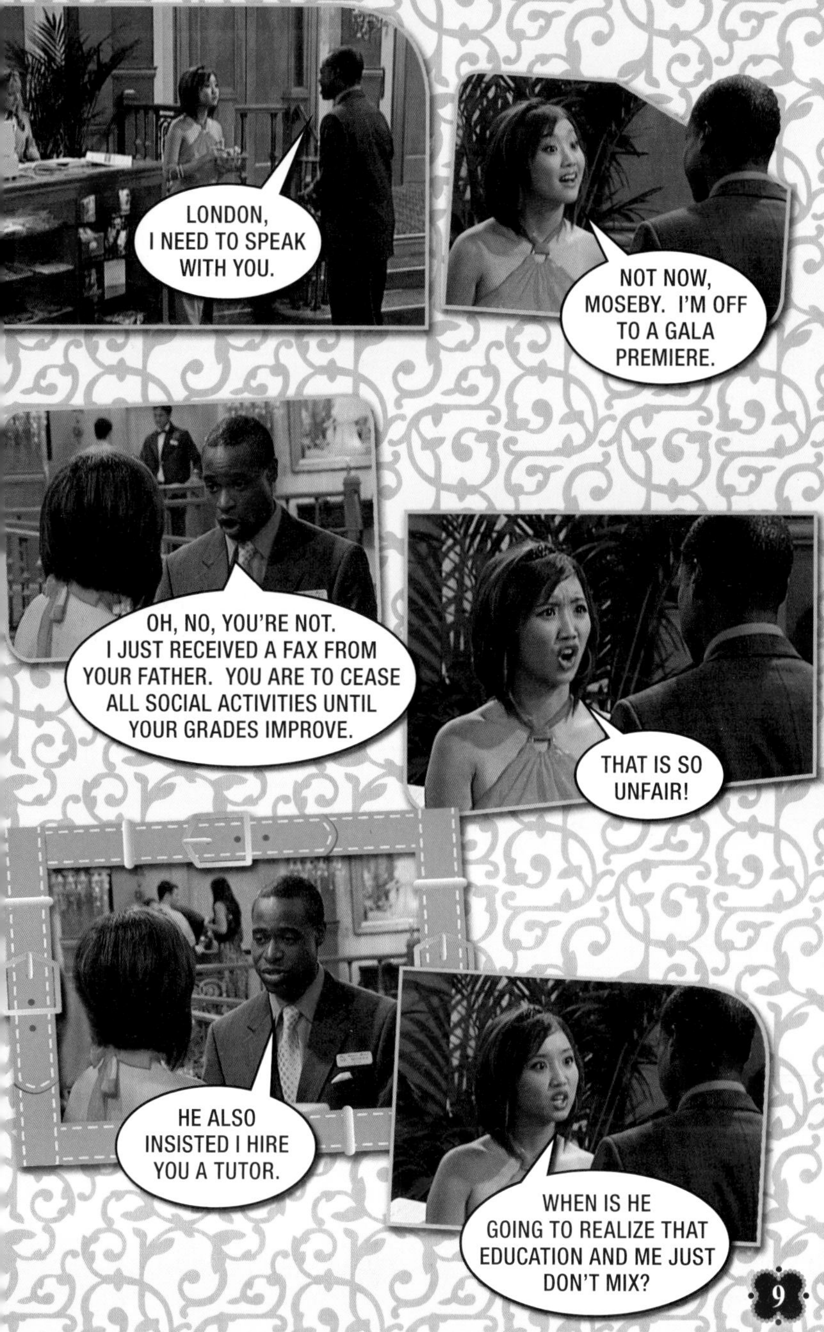
LONDON, I NEED TO SPEAK WITH YOU.
NOT NOW, MOSEBY. I'M OFF TO A GALA PREMIERE.
OH, NO, YOU'RE NOT. I JUST RECEIVED A FAX FROM YOUR FATHER. YOU ARE TO CEASE ALL SOCIAL ACTIVITIES UNTIL YOUR GRADES IMPROVE.
THAT IS SO UNFAIR!
HE ALSO INSISTED I HIRE YOU A TUTOR.
WHEN IS HE GOING TO REALIZE THAT EDUCATION AND ME JUST DON'T MIX?

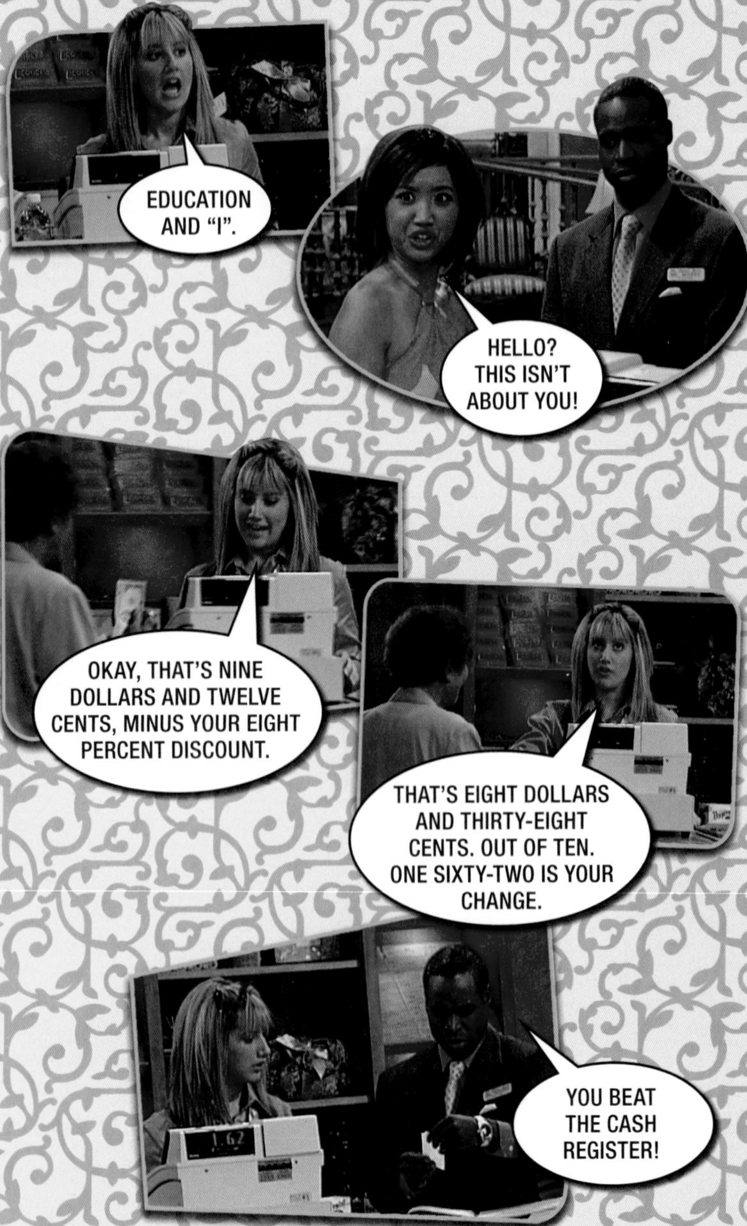
EDUCATION AND "I".
HELLO? THIS ISN'T ABOUT YOU!
OKAY, THAT'S NINE DOLLARS AND TWELVE CENTS, MINUS YOUR EIGHT PERCENT DISCOUNT.
THAT'S EIGHT DOLLARS AND THIRTY-EIGHT CENTS. OUT OF TEN. ONE SIXTY-TWO IS YOUR CHANGE.
1.62
YOU BEAT THE CASH REGISTER!

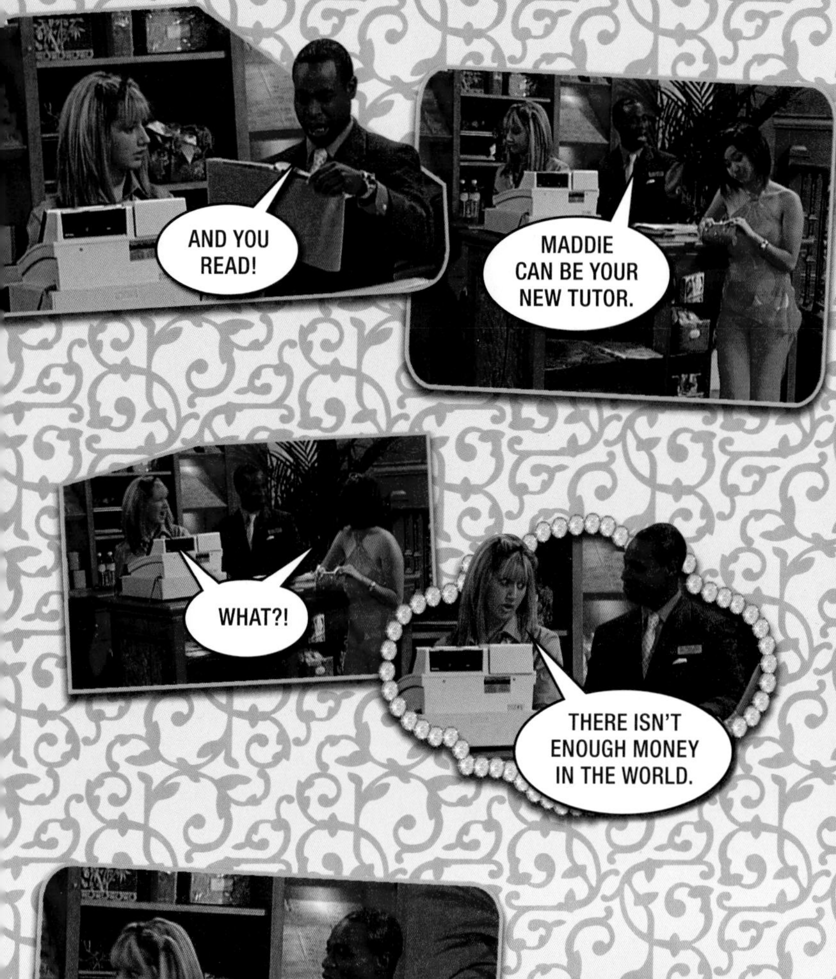
AND YOU READ!
MADDIE CAN BE YOUR NEW TUTOR.
WHAT?!
THERE ISN'T ENOUGH MONEY IN THE WORLD.
I'LL PAY YOU TRIPLE YOUR SALARY.
APPARENTLY THERE IS ENOUGH.

IN THE SCHOOLYARD...

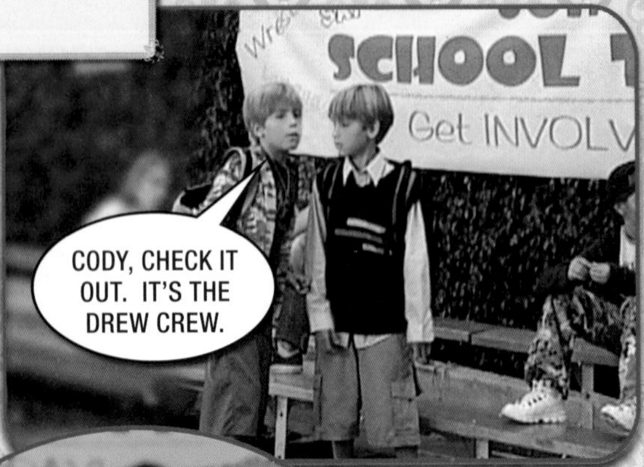
SCHOOL
Get INVOLV
CODY, CHECK IT OUT. IT'S THE DREW CREW.

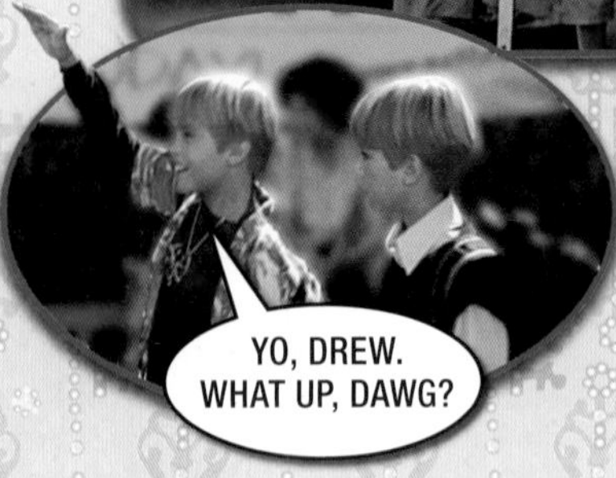
YO, DREW. WHAT UP, DAWG?

DREW CALLS THE TWINS "THE CLONES."

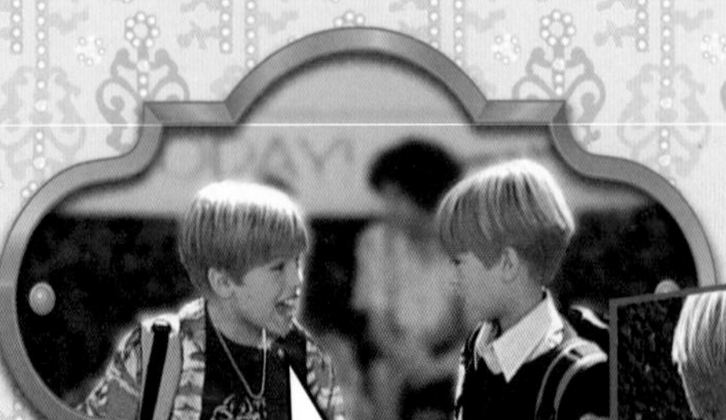
DID YOU HEAR THAT? THE DREW CREW JUST MOCKED US.

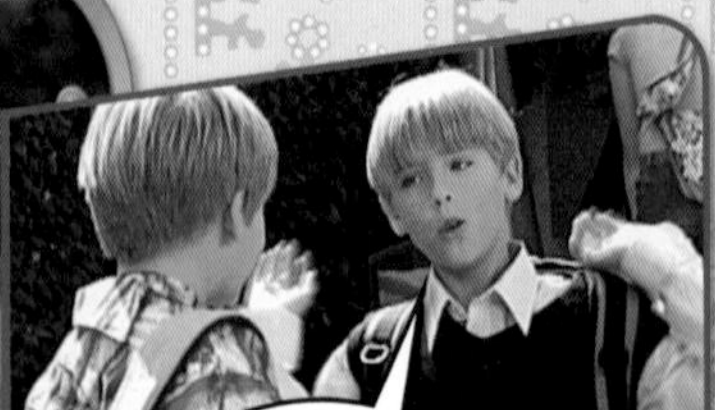
WOO-HOO, WE'RE IN.

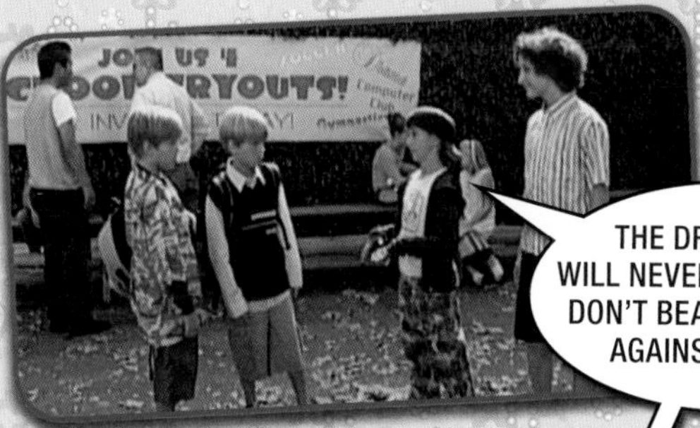
THE DREW CREW WILL NEVER ACCEPT YOU. DON'T BEAT YOUR HEAD AGAINST A WALL.
I'M MAX, BY THE WAY. AND THIS IS TAPEWORM.

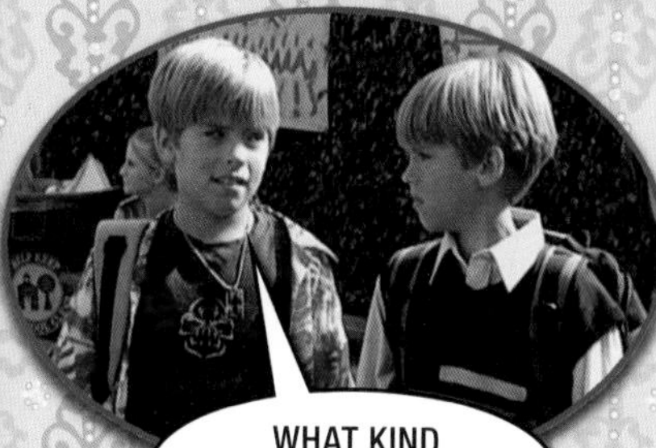
WHAT KIND OF NAME IS THAT?

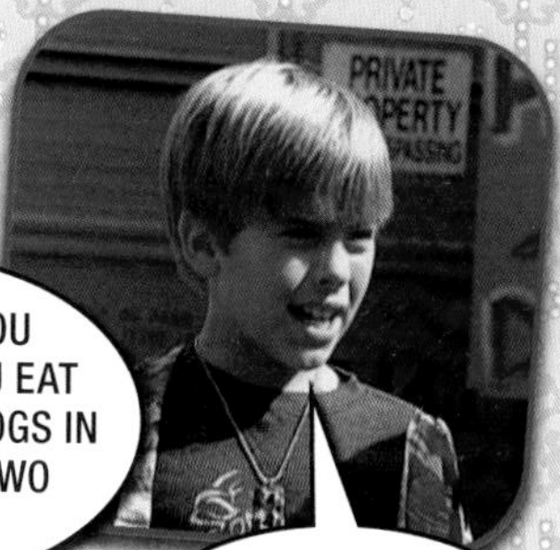
PRIVATE PROPERTY
THE KIND YOU GET WHEN YOU EAT TWENTY HOT DOGS IN LESS THAN TWO MINUTES.
COOL, BEATS MY RECORD.

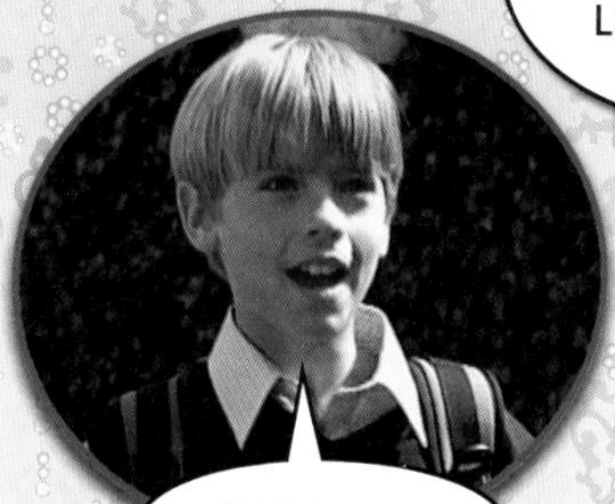
BY EIGHTEEN.

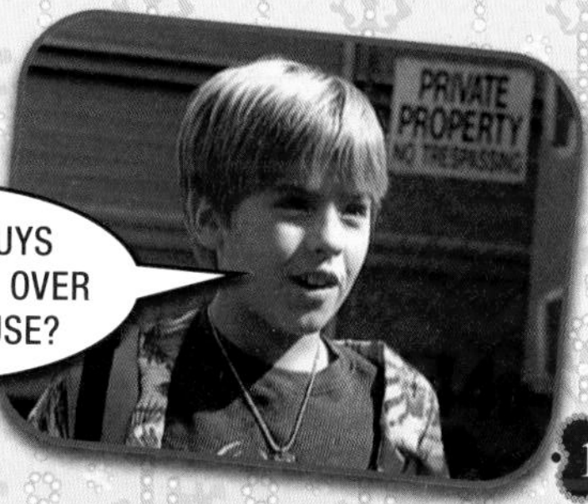
PRIVATE PROPERTY
NO TRESPASSING
HEY, YOU GUYS WANNA COME OVER TO OUR HOUSE?

BACK AT THE HOTEL...

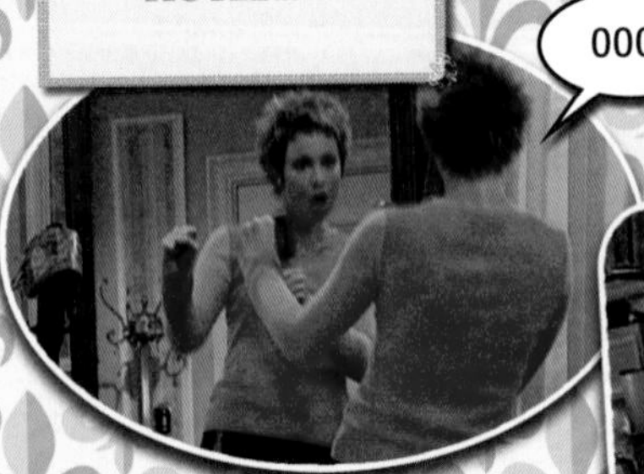
OOO...

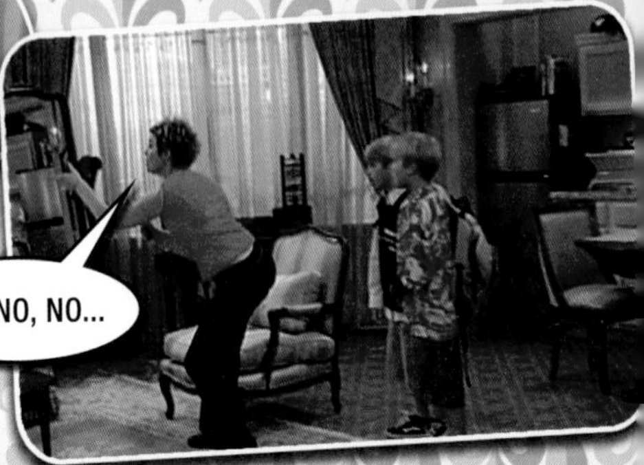
NO, NO, NO...

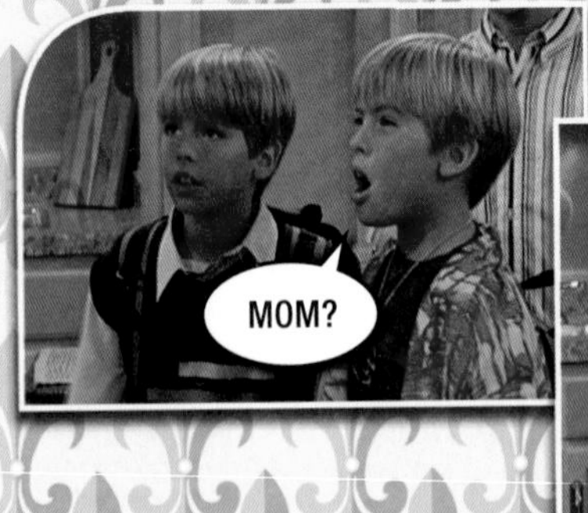
MOM?

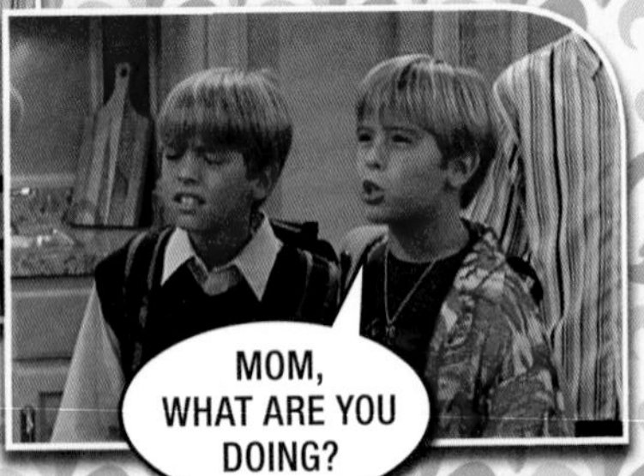
MOM,
WHAT ARE YOU
DOING?

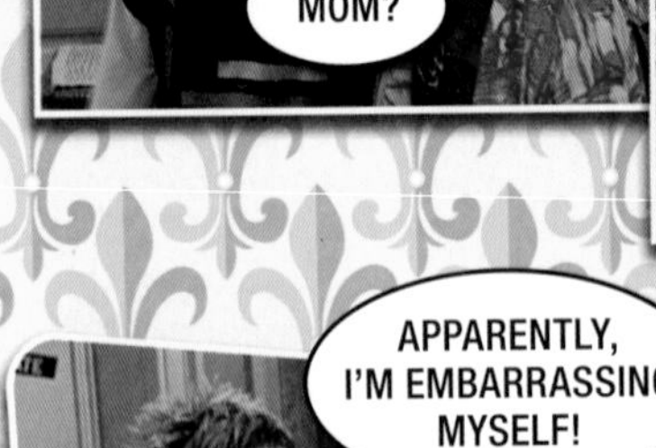
APPARENTLY,
I'M EMBARRASSING
MYSELF!

THE TWINS INTRODUCE THEIR MOM TO MAX AND TAPEWORM, AND MAX SHOWS CAREY SOME DANCE MOVES.

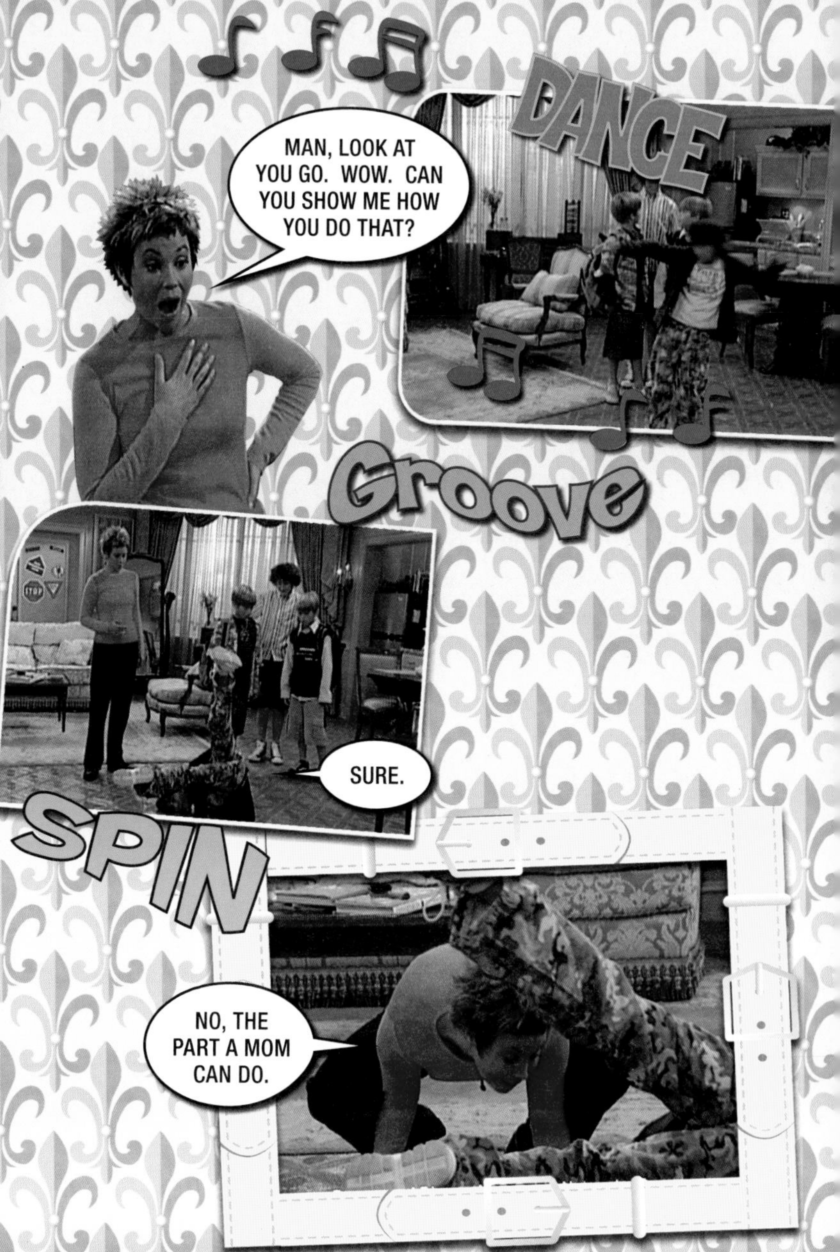
MAN, LOOK AT YOU GO. WOW. CAN YOU SHOW ME HOW YOU DO THAT?
DANCE
Groove
SURE.
SPIN
NO, THE PART A MOM CAN DO.

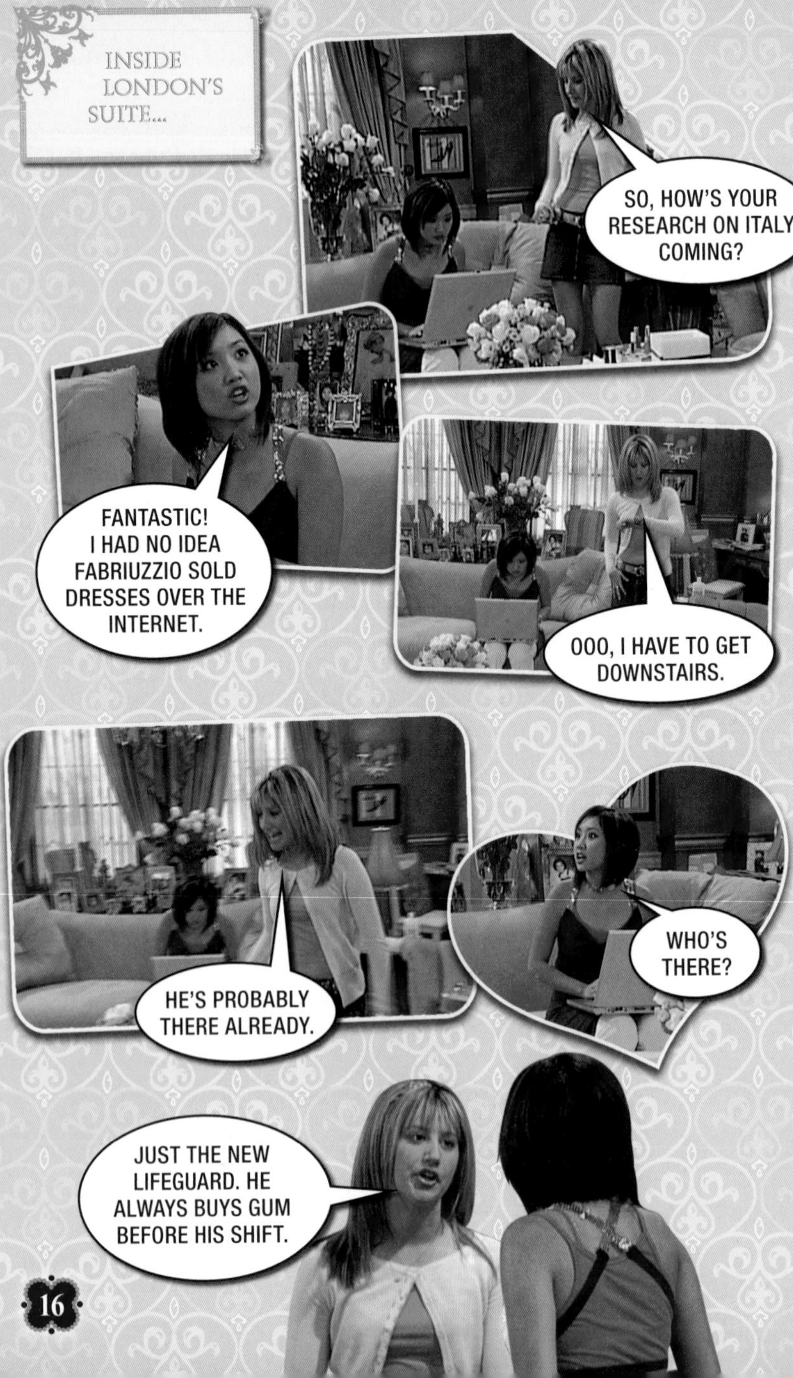
INSIDE LONDON'S SUITE...
SO, HOW'S YOUR RESEARCH ON ITALY COMING?
FANTASTIC! I HAD NO IDEA FABRIUZZIO SOLD DRESSES OVER THE INTERNET.
OOO, I HAVE TO GET DOWNSTAIRS.
HE'S PROBABLY THERE ALREADY.
WHO'S THERE?
JUST THE NEW LIFEGUARD. HE ALWAYS BUYS GUM BEFORE HIS SHIFT.

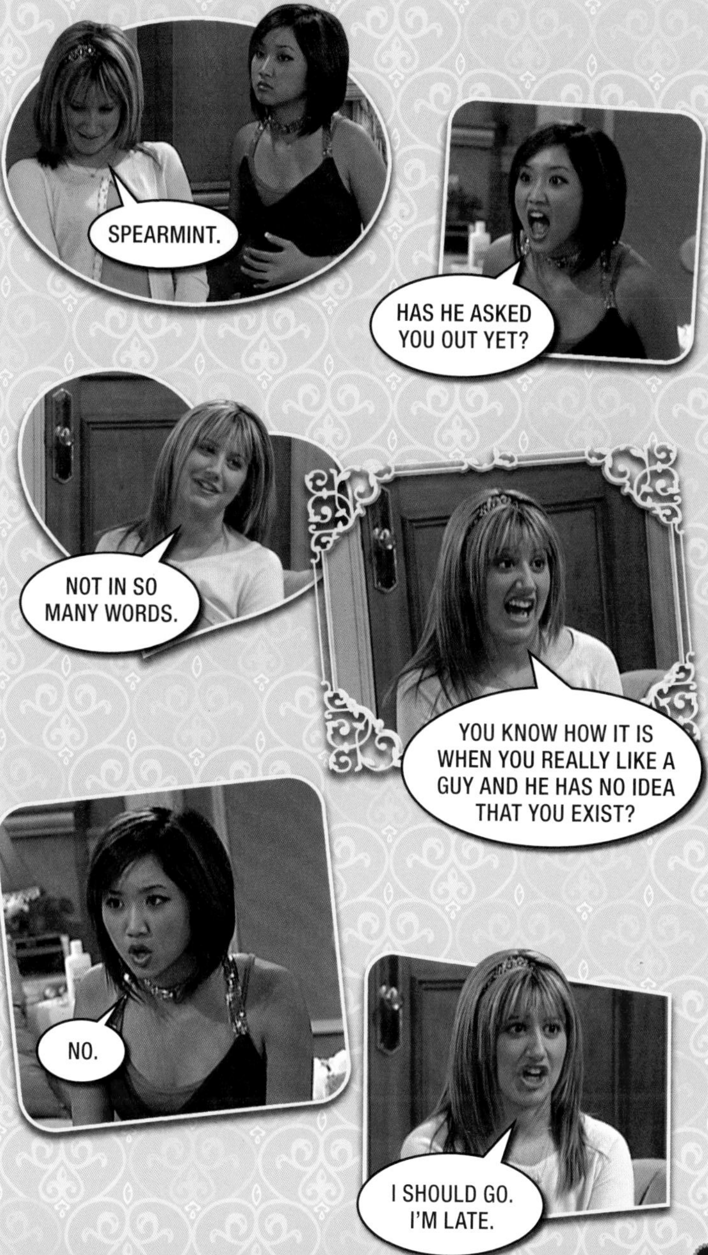
SPEARMINT.
HAS HE ASKED YOU OUT YET?
NOT IN SO MANY WORDS.
YOU KNOW HOW IT IS WHEN YOU REALLY LIKE A GUY AND HE HAS NO IDEA THAT YOU EXIST?
NO.
I SHOULD GO. I'M LATE.

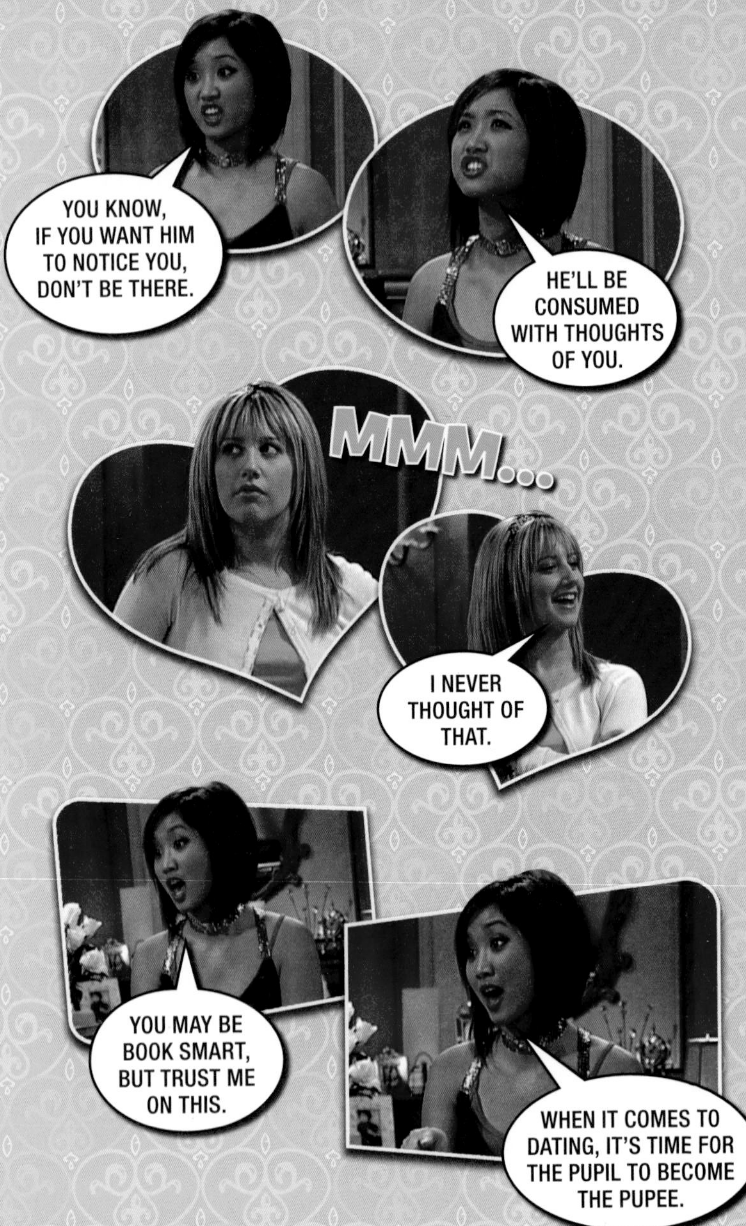
YOU KNOW, IF YOU WANT HIM TO NOTICE YOU, DON'T BE THERE.
HE'LL BE CONSUMED WITH THOUGHTS OF YOU.
MMM...
I NEVER THOUGHT OF THAT.
YOU MAY BE BOOK SMART, BUT TRUST ME ON THIS.
WHEN IT COMES TO DATING, IT'S TIME FOR THE PUPIL TO BECOME THE PUPEE.

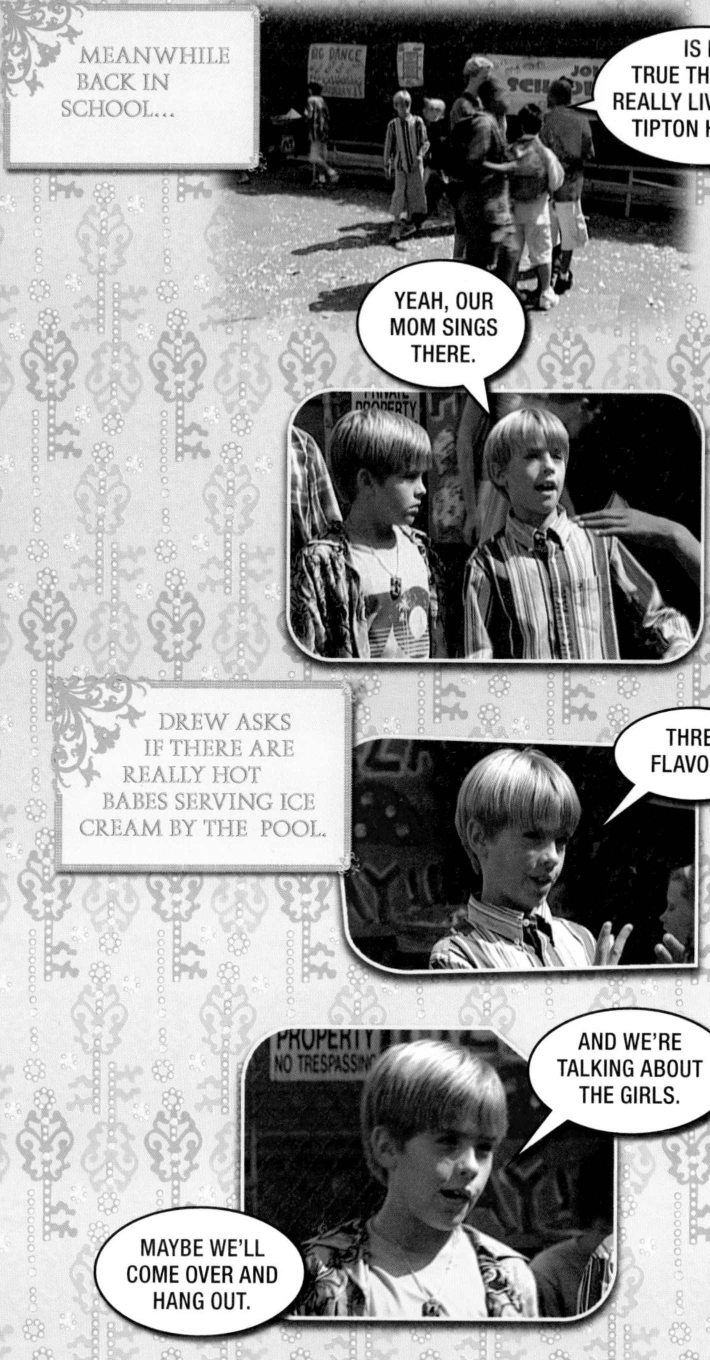
MEANWHILE BACK IN SCHOOL...
IS IT TRUE THAT YOU REALLY LIVE IN THE TIPTON HOTEL?
YEAH, OUR MOM SINGS THERE.
DREW ASKS IF THERE ARE REALLY HOT BABES SERVING ICE CREAM BY THE POOL.
THREE FLAVORS.
AND WE'RE TALKING ABOUT THE GIRLS.
MAYBE WE'LL COME OVER AND HANG OUT.

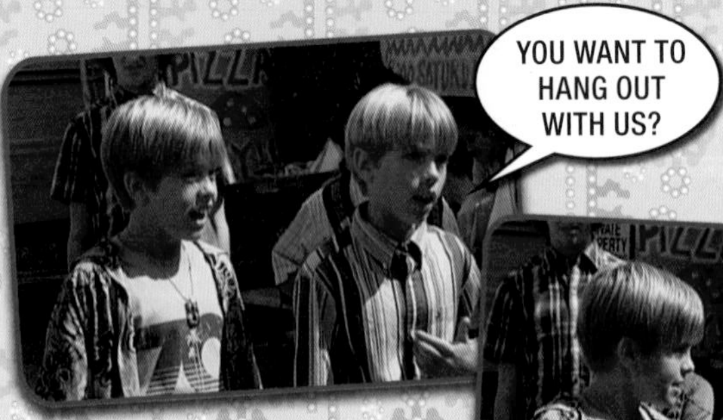
YOU WANT TO HANG OUT WITH US?

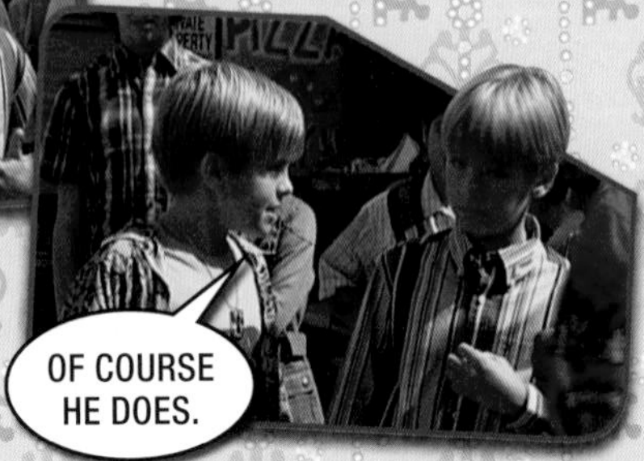
OF COURSE HE DOES.

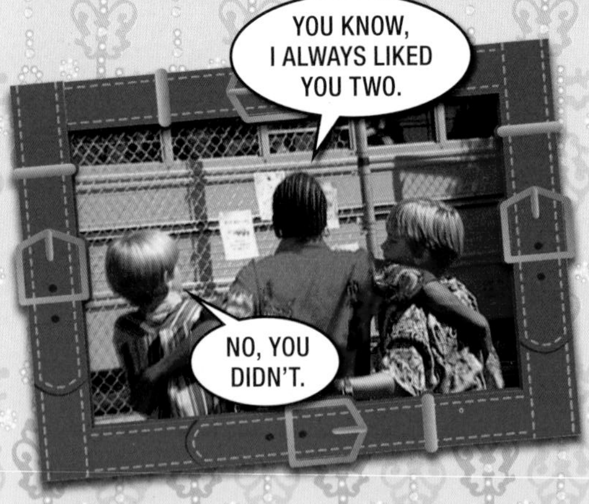
YOU KNOW, I ALWAYS LIKED YOU TWO.
NO, YOU DIDN'T.

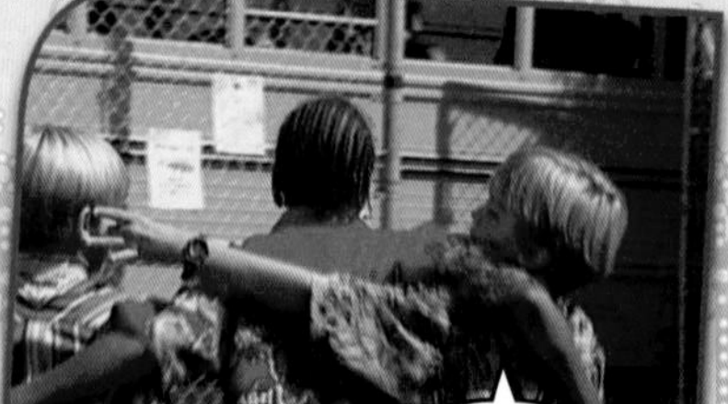
QUIT IT.

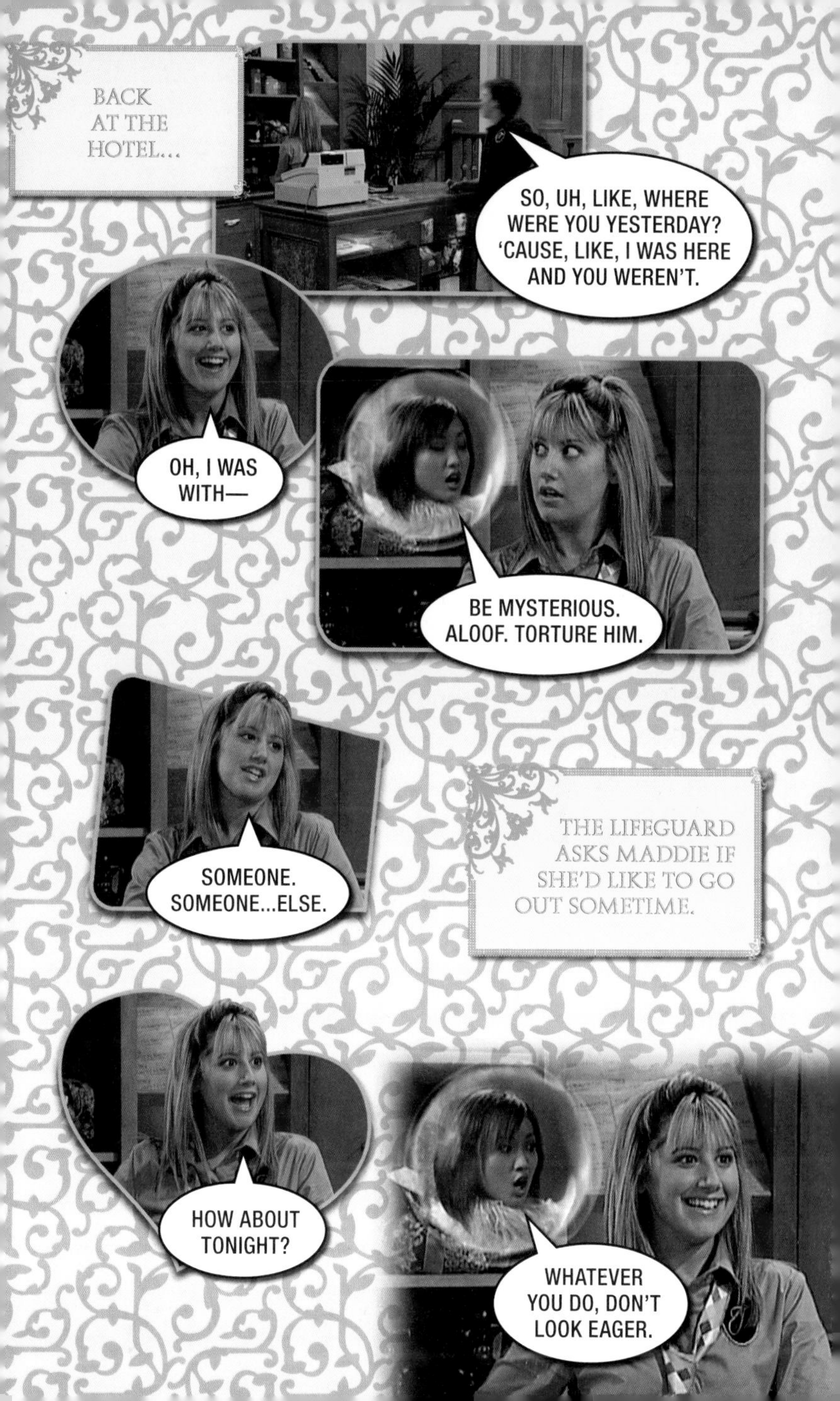
BACK AT THE HOTEL...
SO, UH, LIKE, WHERE WERE YOU YESTERDAY? 'CAUSE, LIKE, I WAS HERE AND YOU WEREN'T.
OH, I WAS WITH—
BE MYSTERIOUS. ALOOF. TORTURE HIM.
SOMEONE. SOMEONE...ELSE.
THE LIFEGUARD ASKS MADDIE IF SHE'D LIKE TO GO OUT SOMETIME.
HOW ABOUT TONIGHT?
WHATEVER YOU DO, DON'T LOOK EAGER.

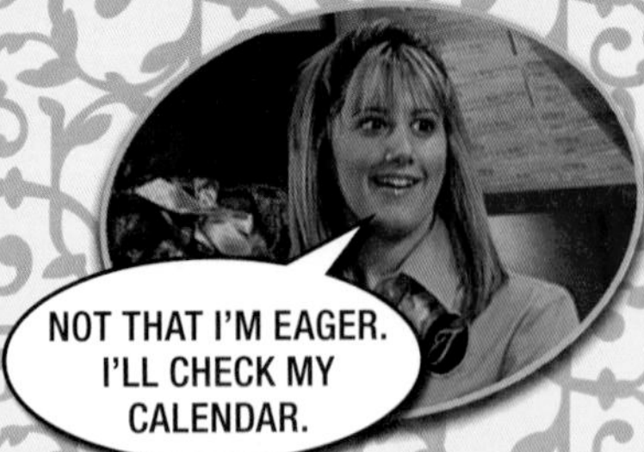
NOT THAT I'M EAGER. I'LL CHECK MY CALENDAR.

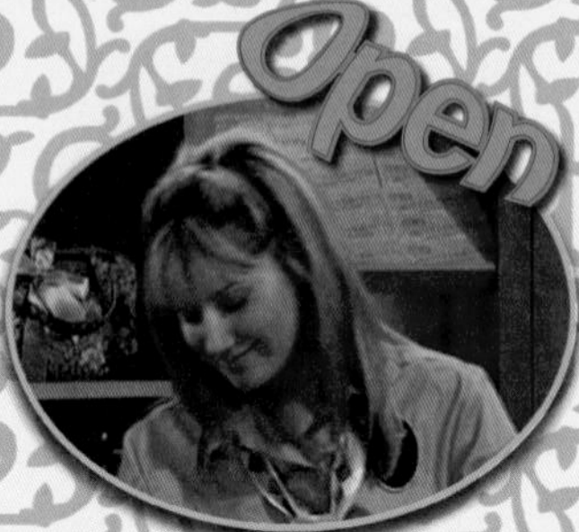
Open

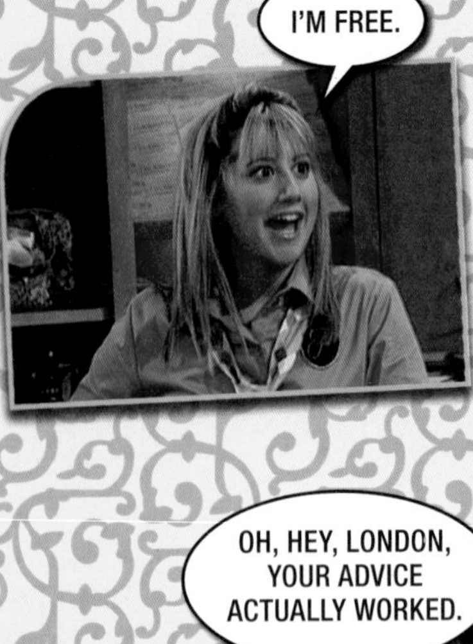
I'M FREE.

THEY MAKE PLANS TO HAVE DINNER AT THE SEAPORT, THEN LANCE THE LIFEGUARD DEPARTS.

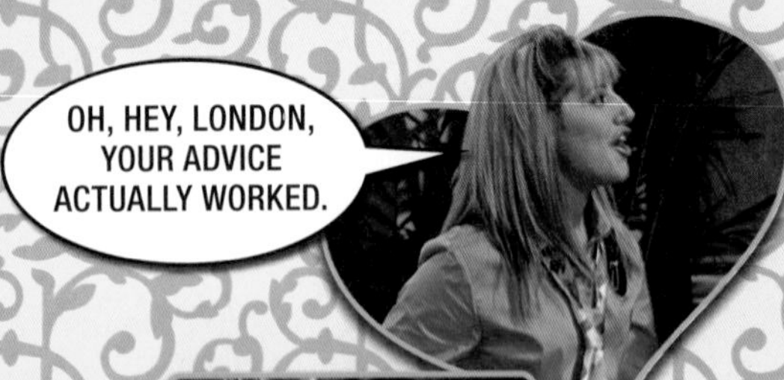
OH, HEY, LONDON, YOUR ADVICE ACTUALLY WORKED.

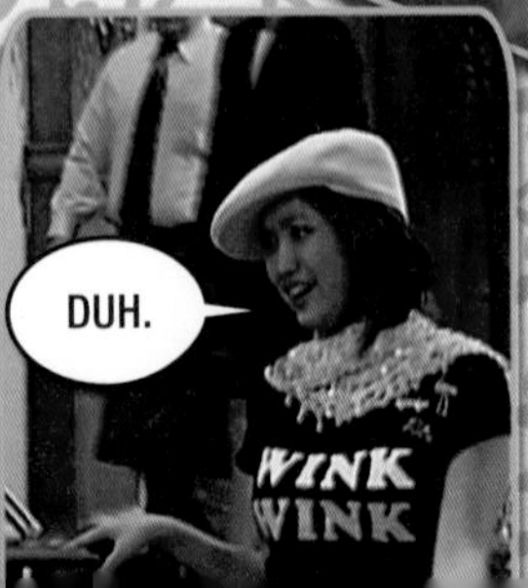
DUH.
WINK
WINK

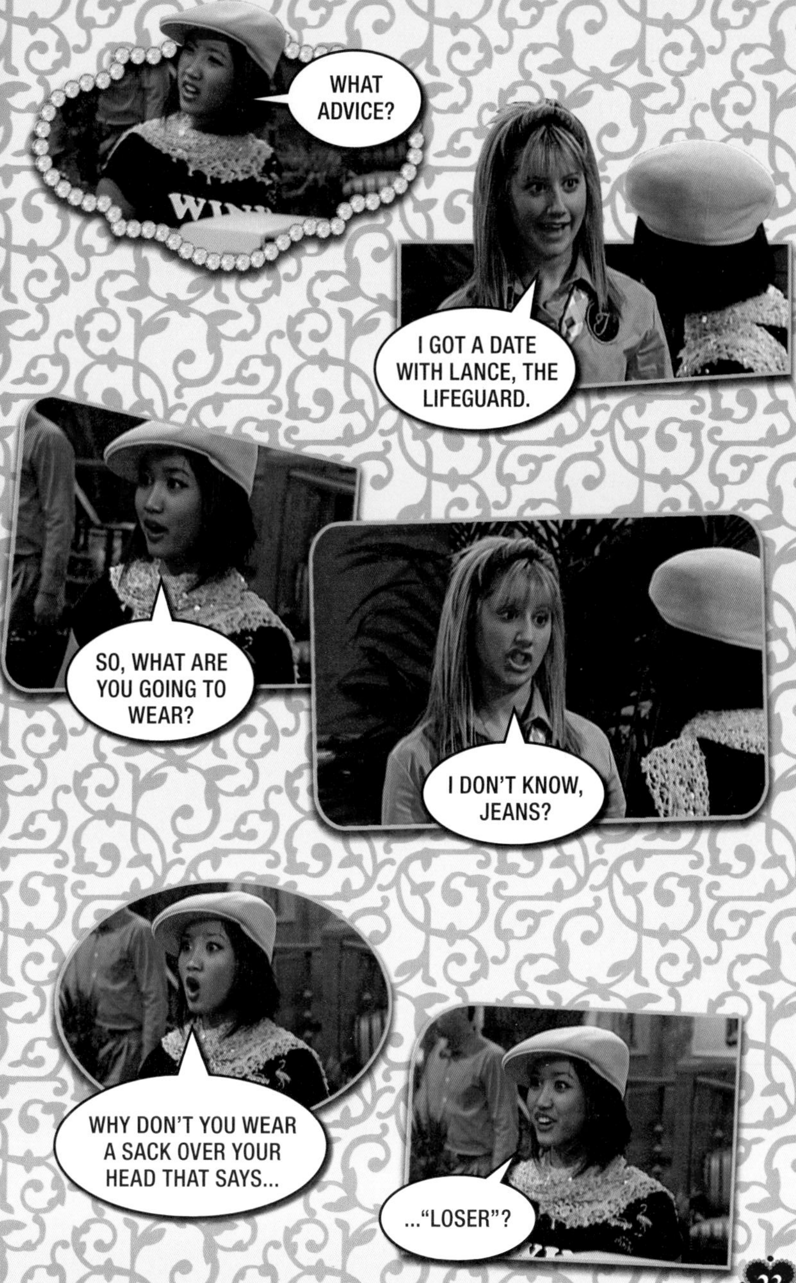
WHAT ADVICE?
I GOT A DATE WITH LANCE, THE LIFEGUARD.
SO, WHAT ARE YOU GOING TO WEAR?
I DON'T KNOW, JEANS?
WHY DON'T YOU WEAR A SACK OVER YOUR HEAD THAT SAYS...
..."LOSER"?

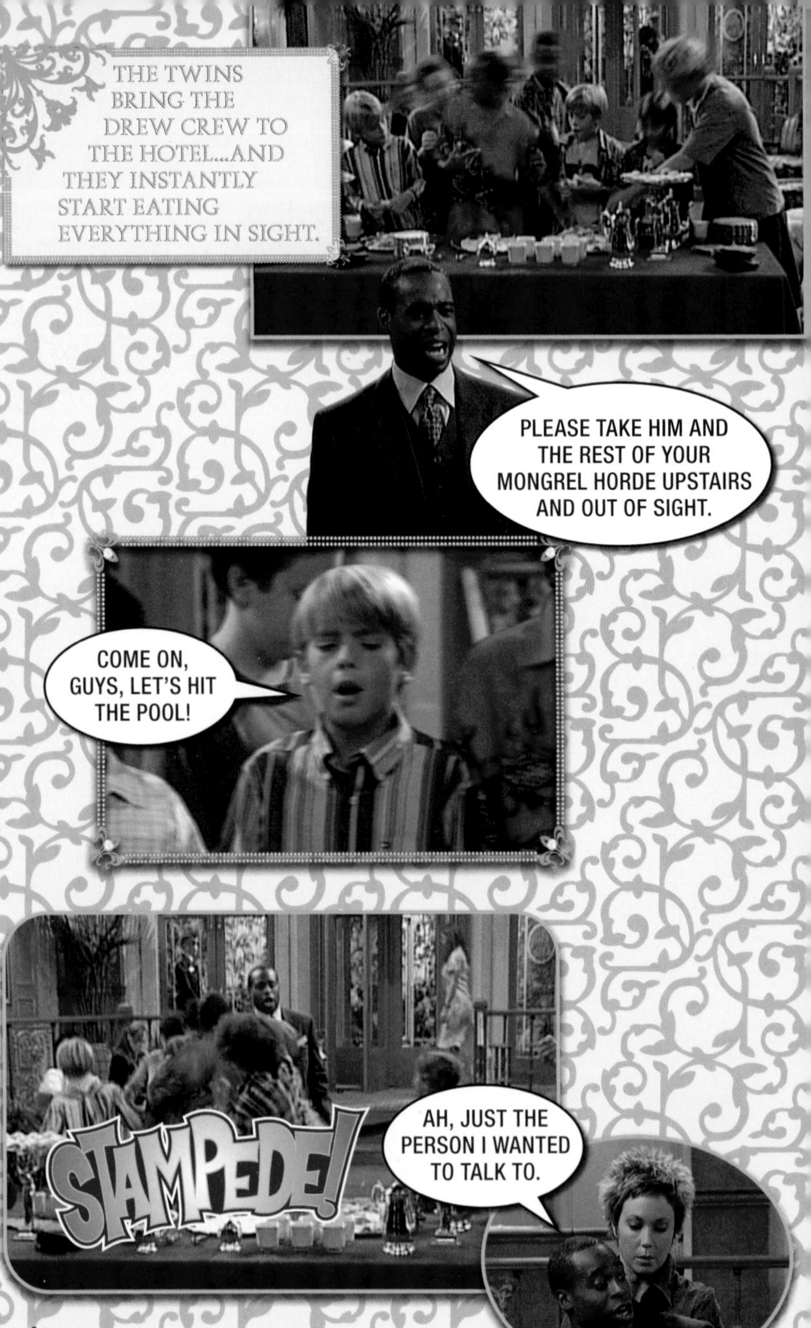
THE TWINS BRING THE DREW CREW TO THE HOTEL...AND THEY INSTANTLY START EATING EVERYTHING IN SIGHT.
PLEASE TAKE HIM AND THE REST OF YOUR MONGREL HORDE UPSTAIRS AND OUT OF SIGHT.
COME ON, GUYS, LET'S HIT THE POOL!
STAMPEDE!
AH, JUST THE PERSON I WANTED TO TALK TO.

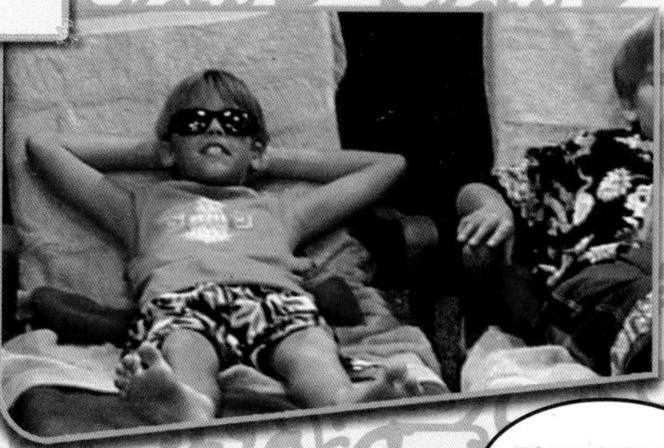
AT THE ROOFTOP POOL...

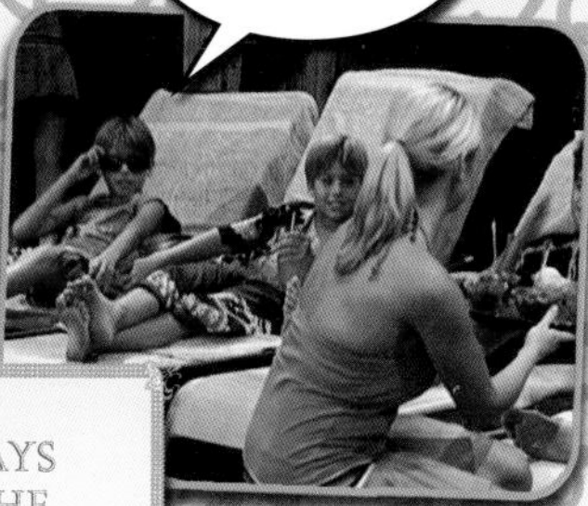
FOUR O'CLOCK ICE CREAM.
DREW SAYS MAYBE THE TWINS AREN'T SO LAME AFTER ALL.

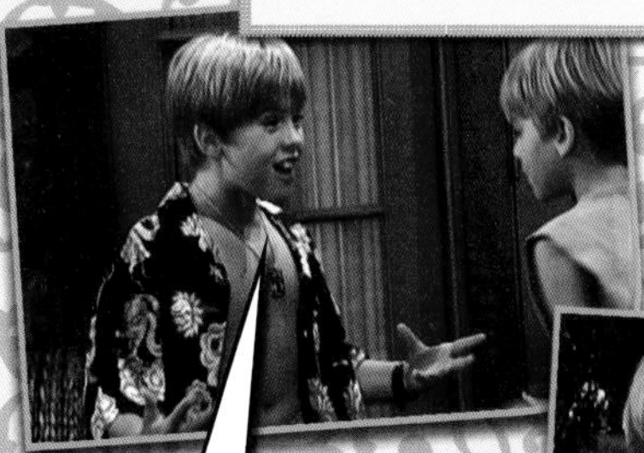
DID YOU HEAR THAT? WE'RE IN! WE'RE NOT SO LAME.

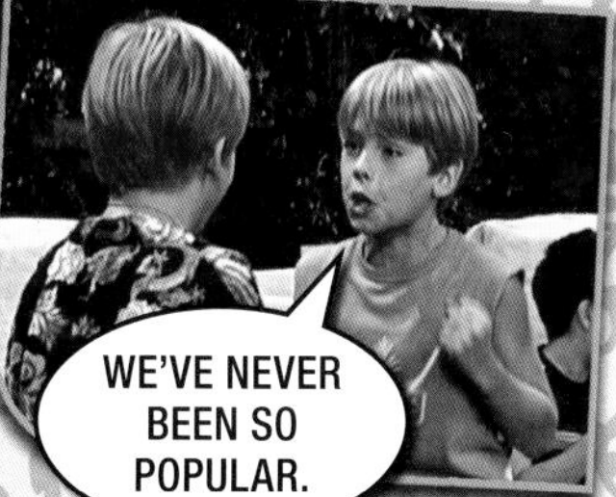
WE'VE NEVER BEEN SO POPULAR.

THE DREW CREW IS RUDE TO MAX AND TAPEWORM... AND DREW SOON SAYS, "HEY, YA'LL, LET'S DITCH THE DWEEBS."

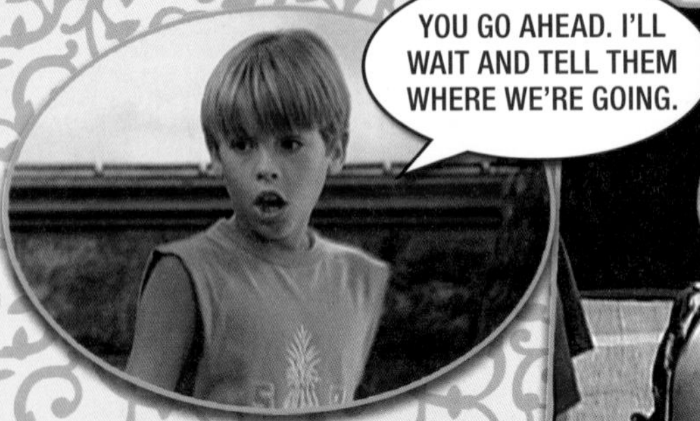
YOU GO AHEAD. I'LL WAIT AND TELL THEM WHERE WE'RE GOING.

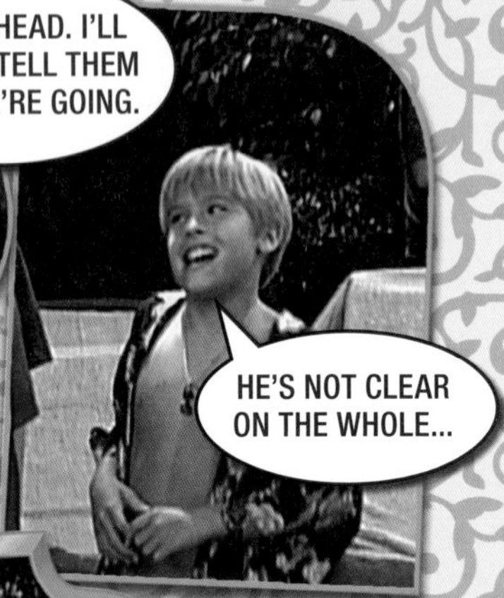
HE'S NOT CLEAR ON THE WHOLE...

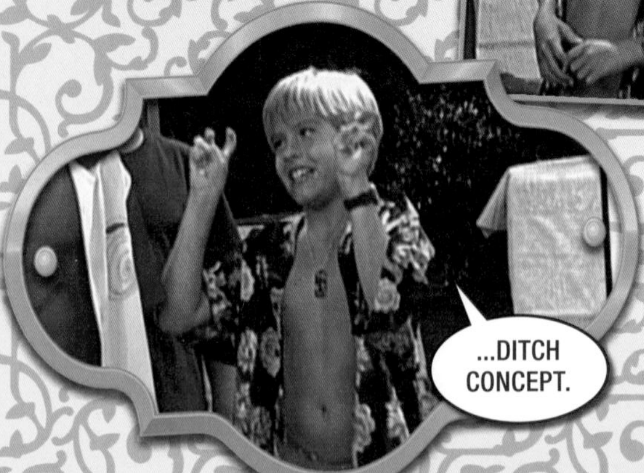
...DITCH CONCEPT.

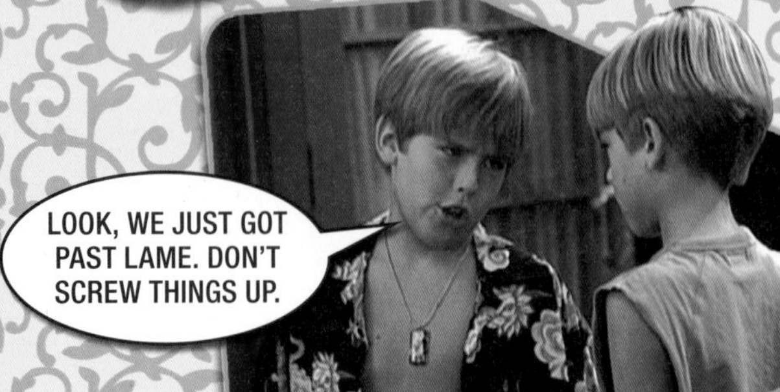
LOOK, WE JUST GOT PAST LAME. DON'T SCREW THINGS UP.

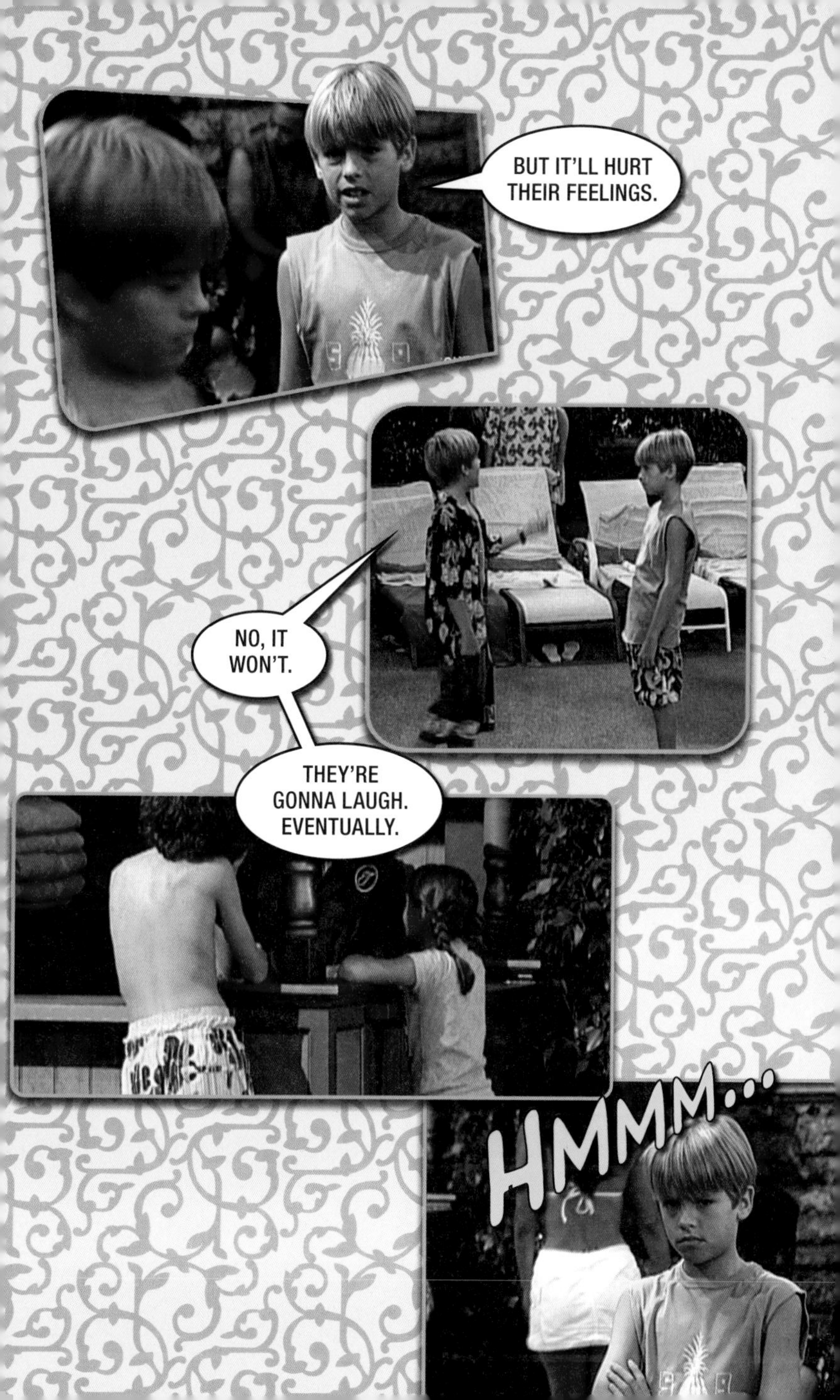
BUT IT'LL HURT THEIR FEELINGS.
NO, IT WON'T.
THEY'RE GONNA LAUGH. EVENTUALLY.
HMMM...

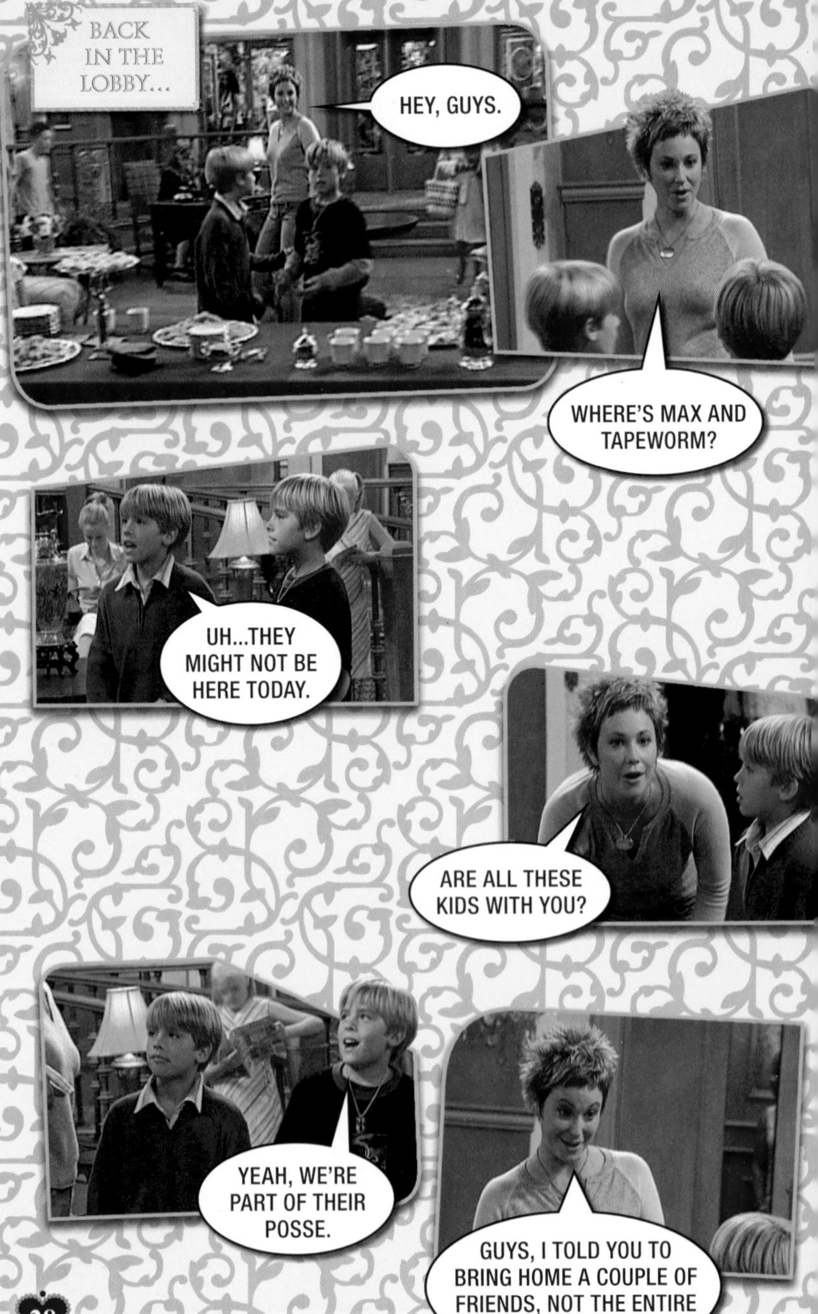
BACK IN THE LOBBY...
HEY, GUYS.
WHERE'S MAX AND TAPEWORM?
UH...THEY MIGHT NOT BE HERE TODAY.
ARE ALL THESE KIDS WITH YOU?
YEAH, WE'RE PART OF THEIR POSSE.
GUYS, I TOLD YOU TO BRING HOME A COUPLE OF FRIENDS, NOT THE ENTIRE SCHOOL! FIX IT!

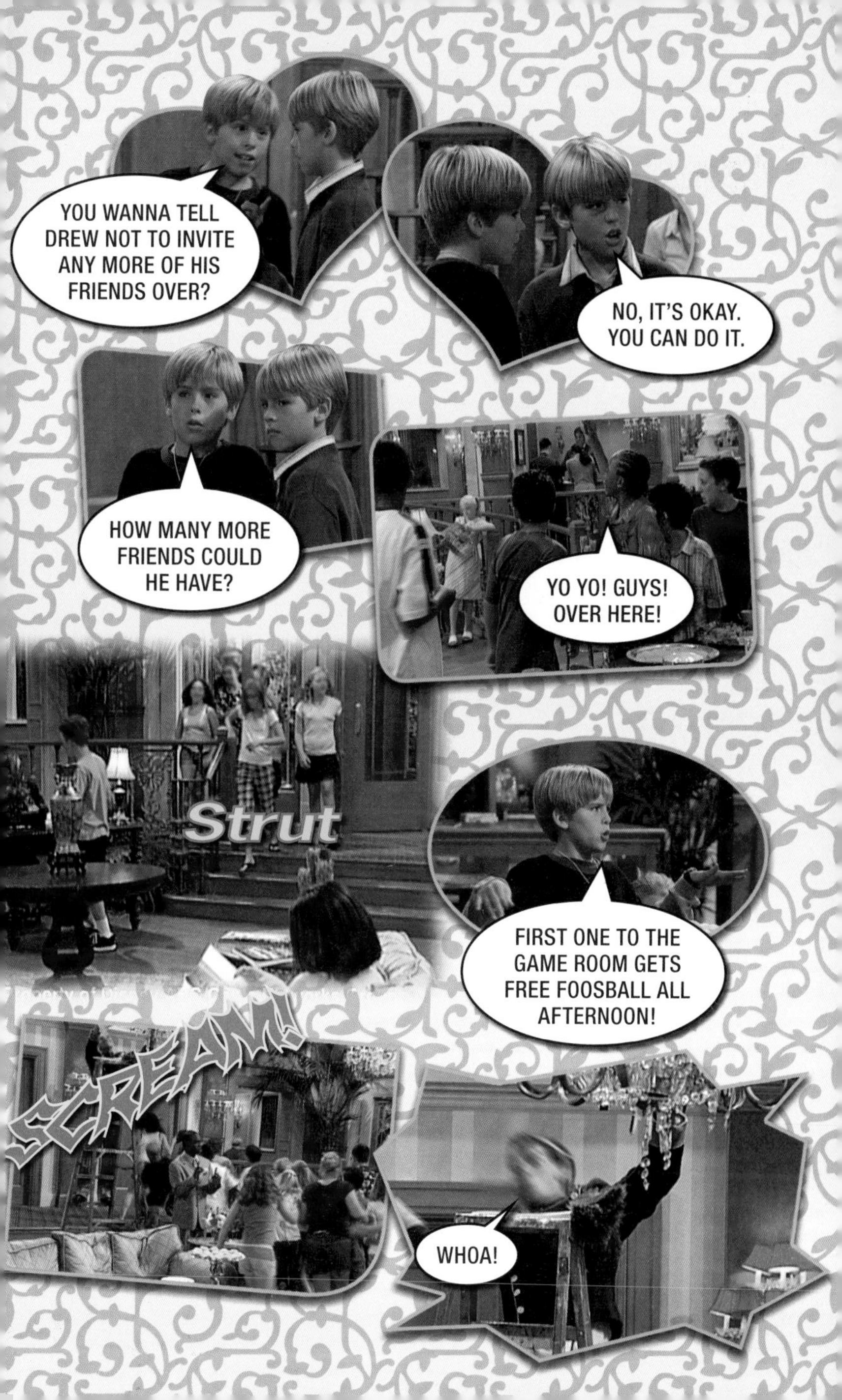
YOU WANNA TELL DREW NOT TO INVITE ANY MORE OF HIS FRIENDS OVER?
NO, IT'S OKAY. YOU CAN DO IT.
HOW MANY MORE FRIENDS COULD HE HAVE?
YO YO! GUYS! OVER HERE!
Strut
FIRST ONE TO THE GAME ROOM GETS FREE FOOSBALL ALL AFTERNOON!
SCREAM!
WHOA!

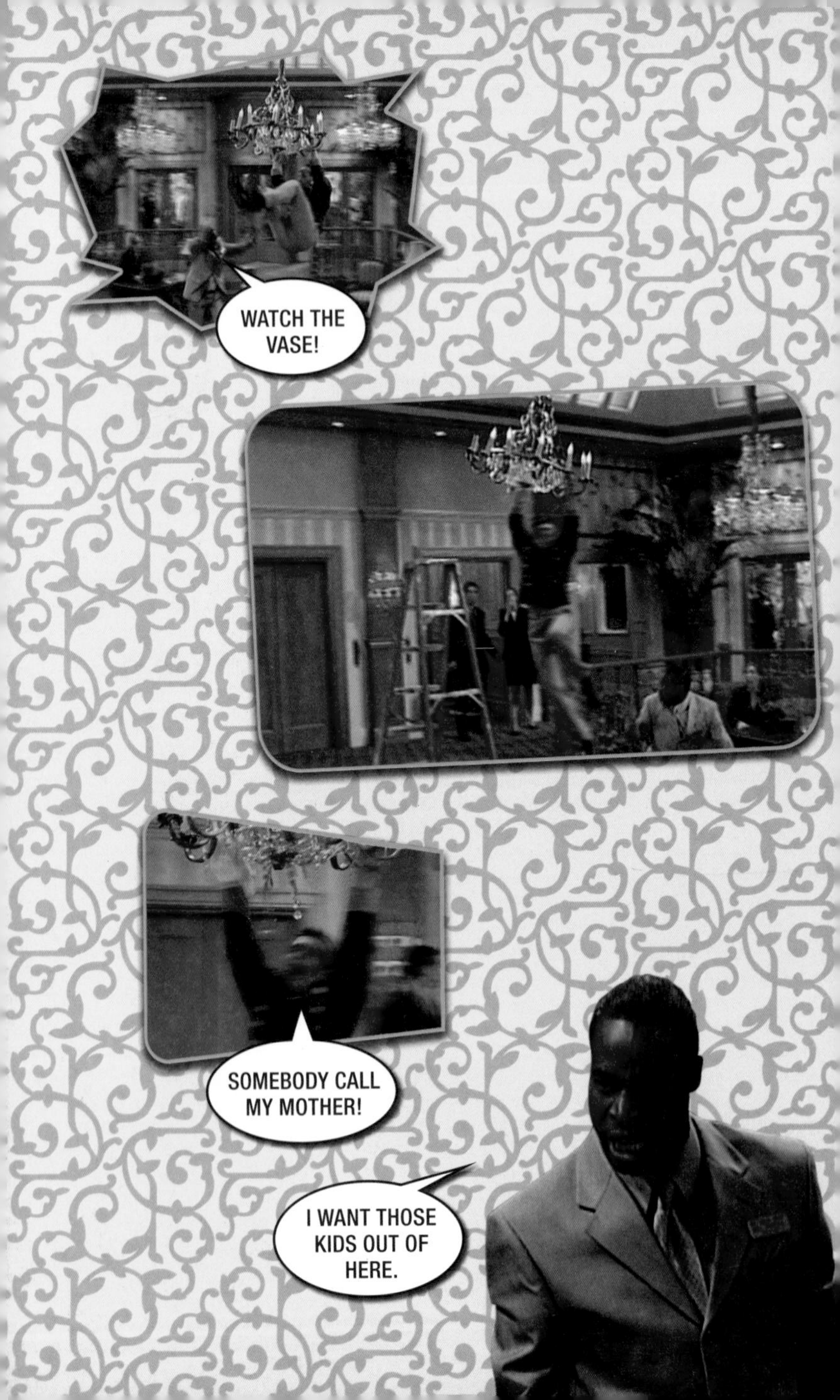
WATCH THE VASE!
SOMEBODY CALL MY MOTHER!
I WANT THOSE KIDS OUT OF HERE.

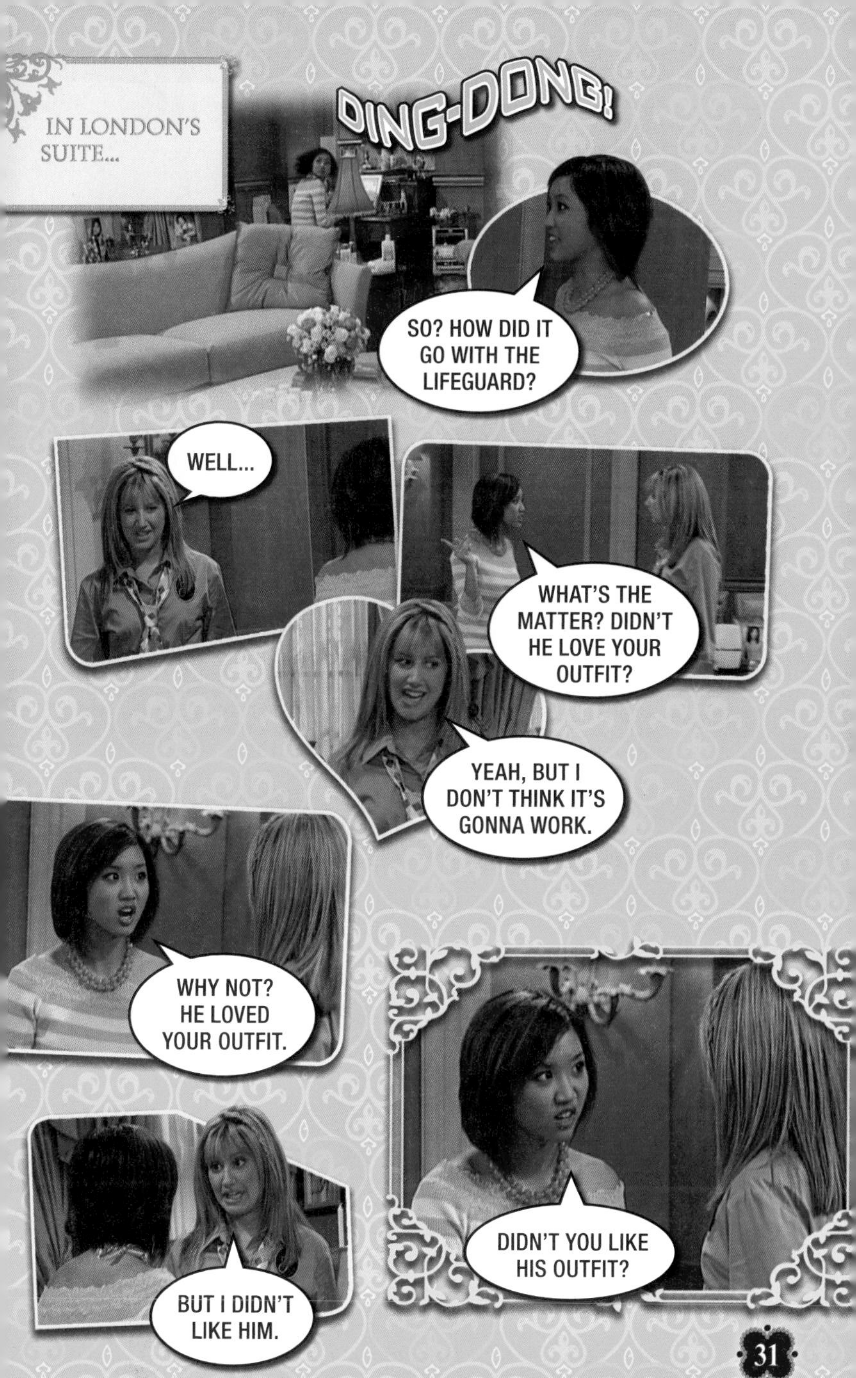
IN LONDON'S SUITE...
DING-DONG!
SO? HOW DID IT GO WITH THE LIFEGUARD?
WELL...
WHAT'S THE MATTER? DIDN'T HE LOVE YOUR OUTFIT?
YEAH, BUT I DON'T THINK IT'S GONNA WORK.
WHY NOT? HE LOVED YOUR OUTFIT.
DIDN'T YOU LIKE HIS OUTFIT?
BUT I DIDN'T LIKE HIM.

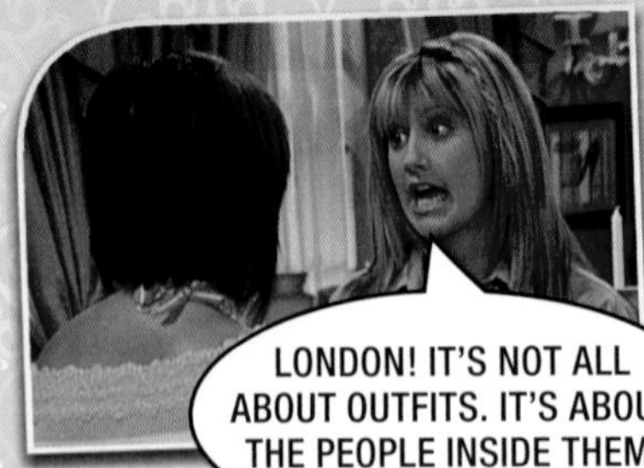
LONDON! IT'S NOT ALL ABOUT OUTFITS. IT'S ABOUT THE PEOPLE INSIDE THEM.
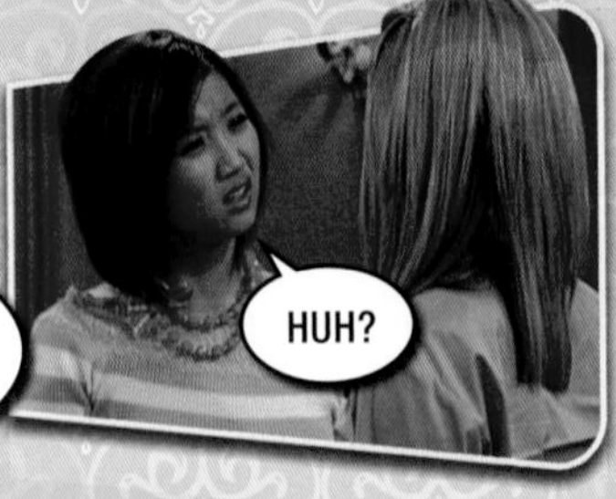
HUH?
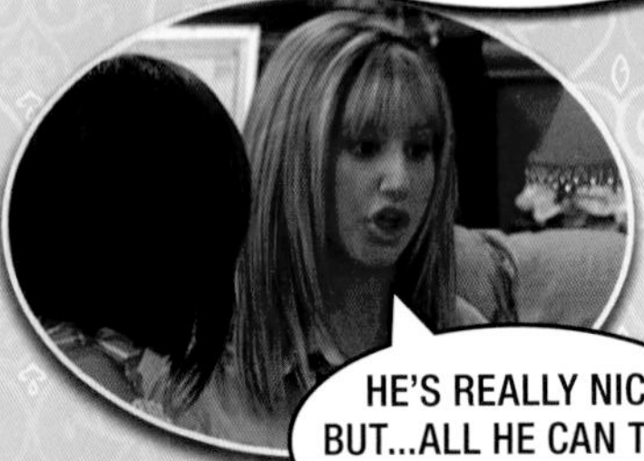
HE'S REALLY NICE BUT...ALL HE CAN TALK ABOUT IS WATER!
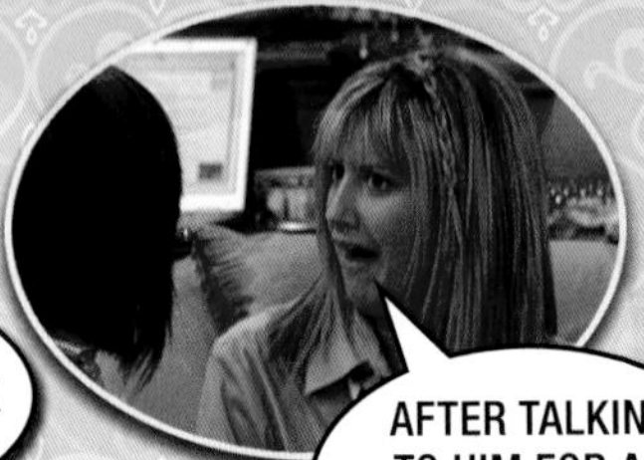
AFTER TALKING TO HIM FOR AN HOUR, I HAD TO GO SO BAD.
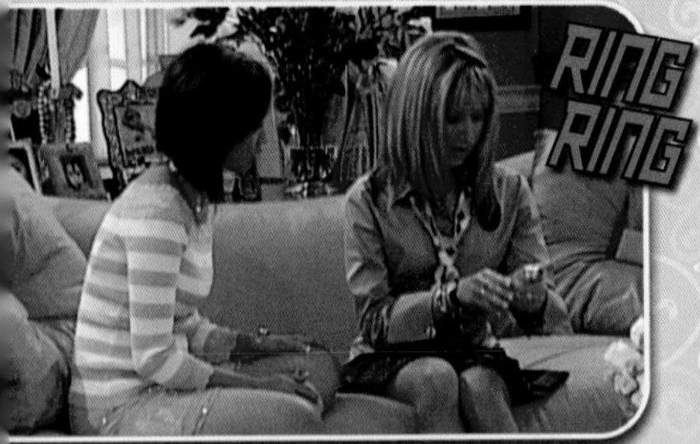
RING RING
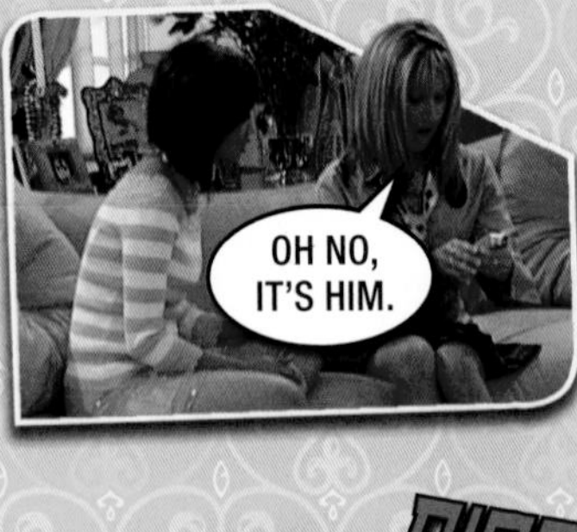
OH NO, IT'S HIM.
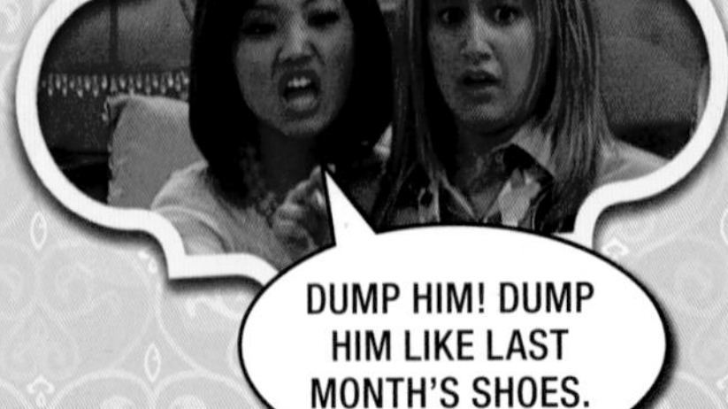
DUMP HIM! DUMP HIM LIKE LAST MONTH'S SHOES.
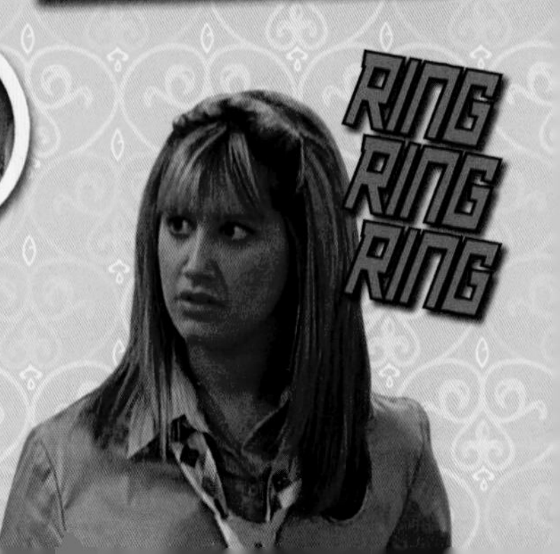
RING RING RING

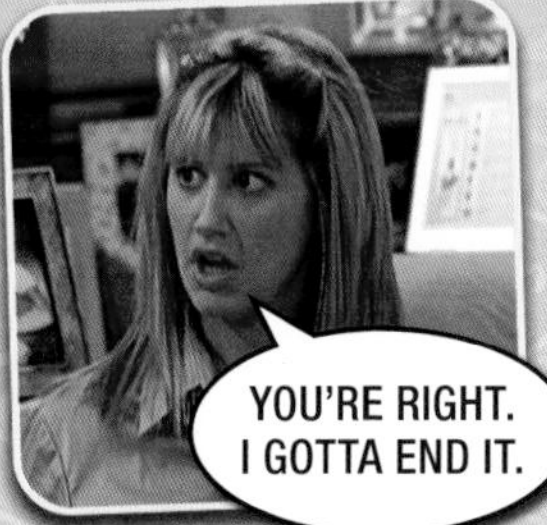
YOU'RE RIGHT. I GOTTA END IT.
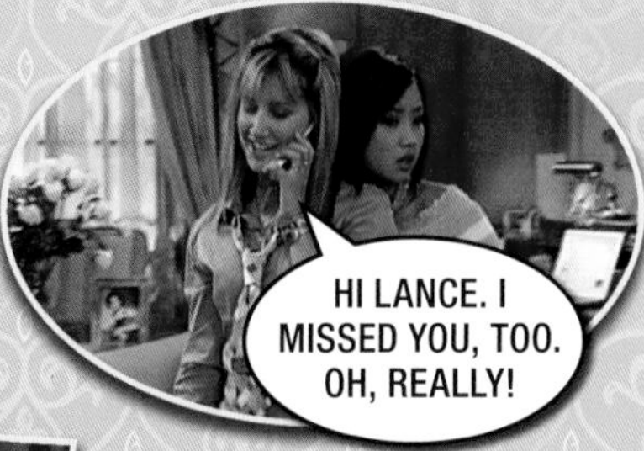
HI LANCE. I MISSED YOU, TOO. OH, REALLY!
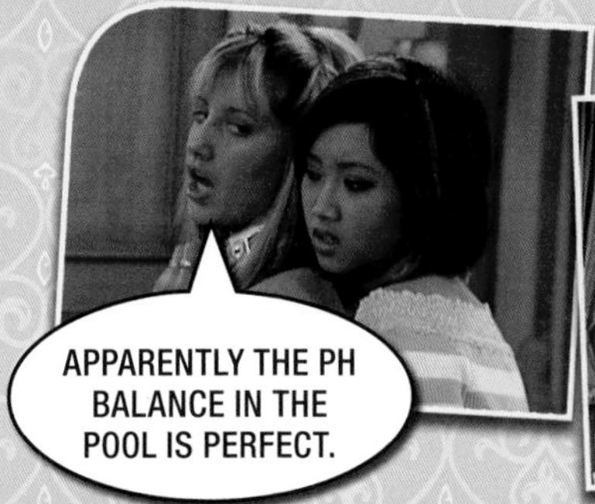
APPARENTLY THE PH BALANCE IN THE POOL IS PERFECT.
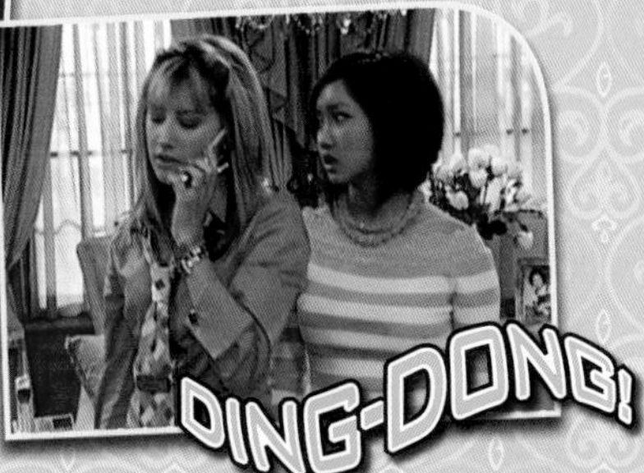
DING-DONG!
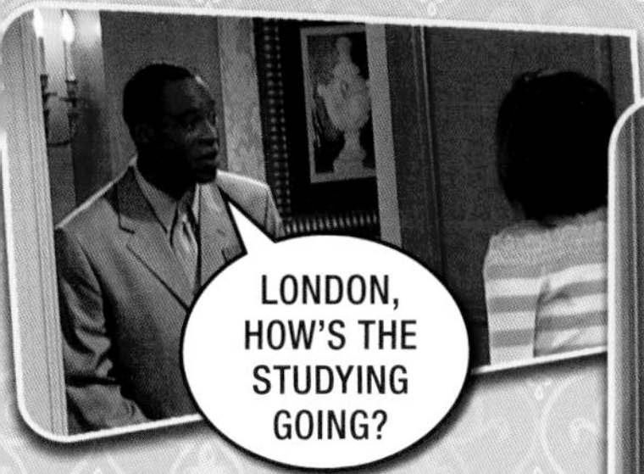
LONDON, HOW'S THE STUDYING GOING?
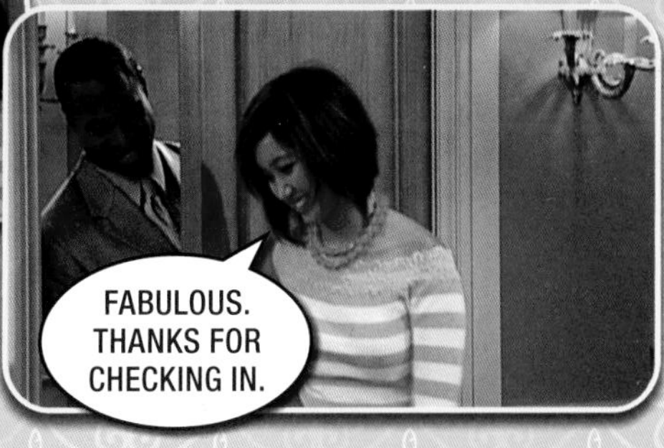
FABULOUS. THANKS FOR CHECKING IN.
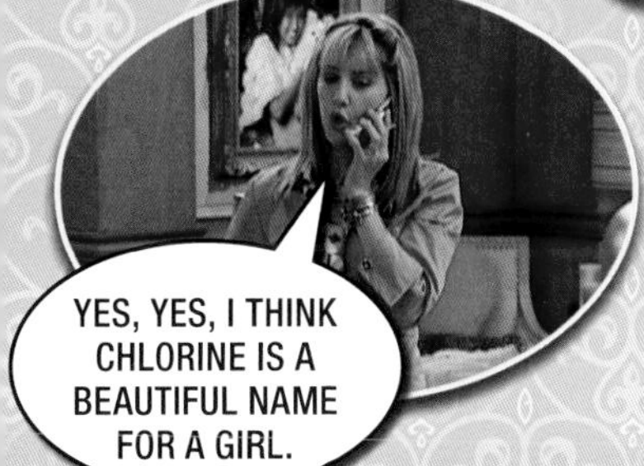
YES, YES, I THINK CHLORINE IS A BEAUTIFUL NAME FOR A GIRL.
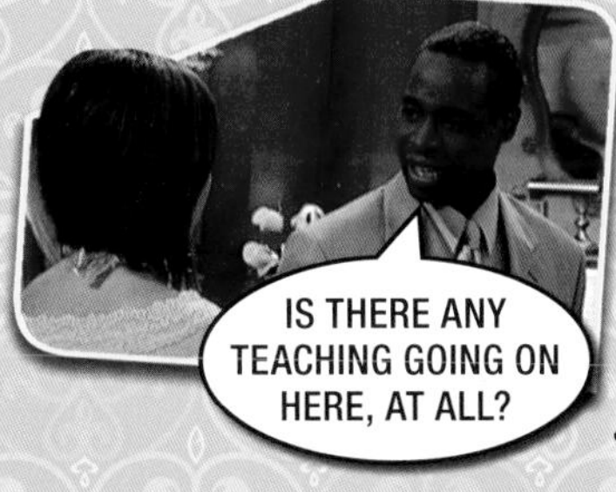
IS THERE ANY TEACHING GOING ON HERE, AT ALL?

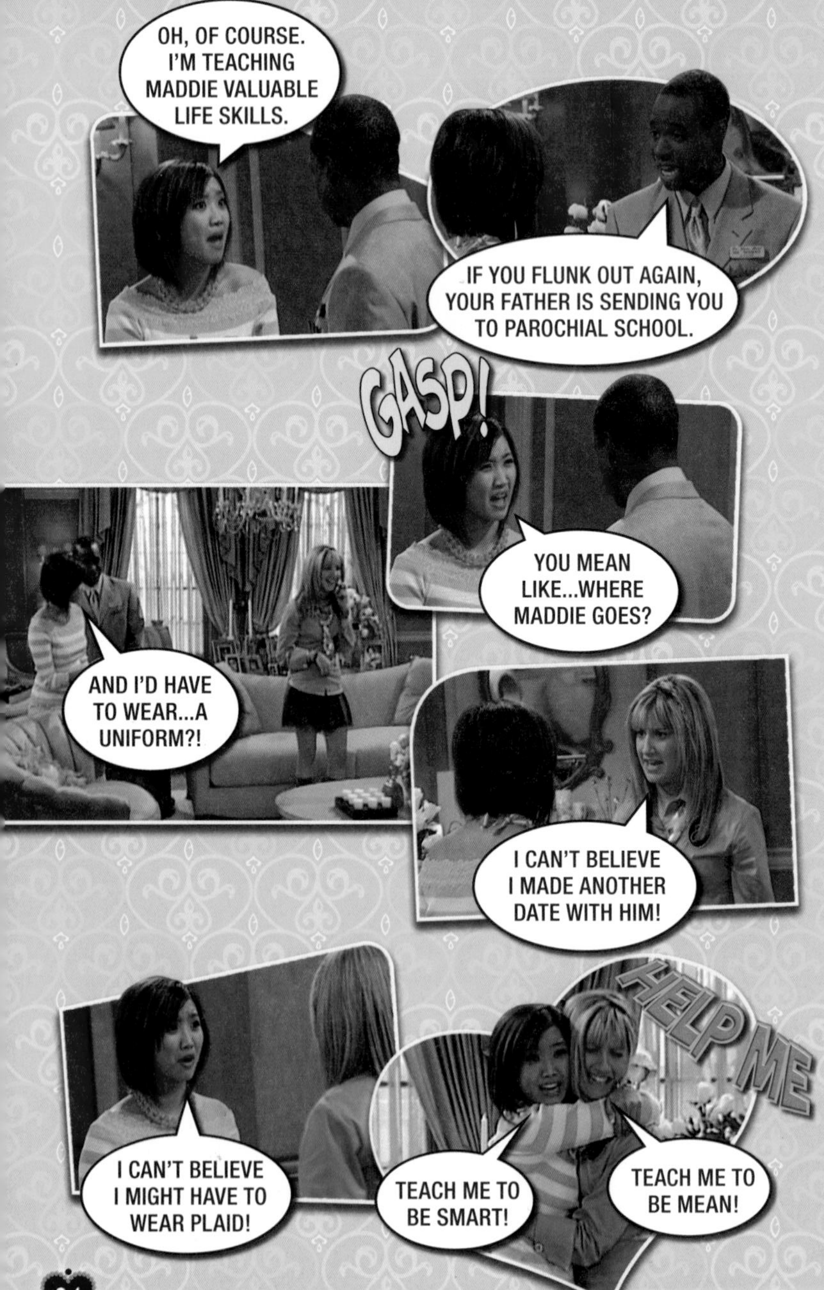

OH, OF COURSE. I'M TEACHING MADDIE VALUABLE LIFE SKILLS.
IF YOU FLUNK OUT AGAIN, YOUR FATHER IS SENDING YOU TO PAROCHIAL SCHOOL.
GASP!
YOU MEAN LIKE...WHERE MADDIE GOES?
AND I'D HAVE TO WEAR...A UNIFORM?!
I CAN'T BELIEVE I MADE ANOTHER DATE WITH HIM!
I CAN'T BELIEVE I MIGHT HAVE TO WEAR PLAID!
TEACH ME TO BE SMART!
HELP ME
TEACH ME TO BE MEAN!

IN THE GAME ROOM...

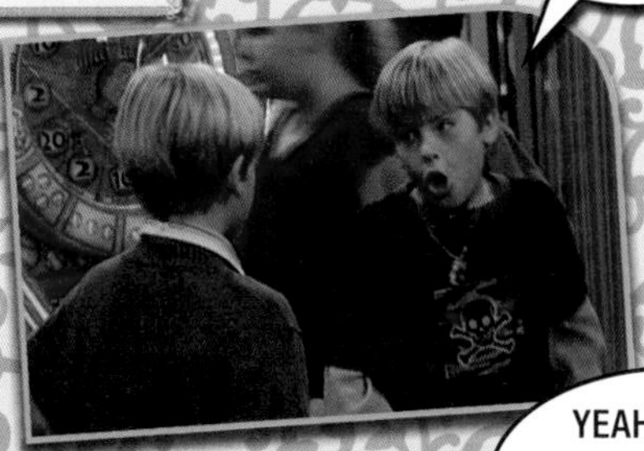
ALL OF THE A-LIST KIDS ARE HERE.

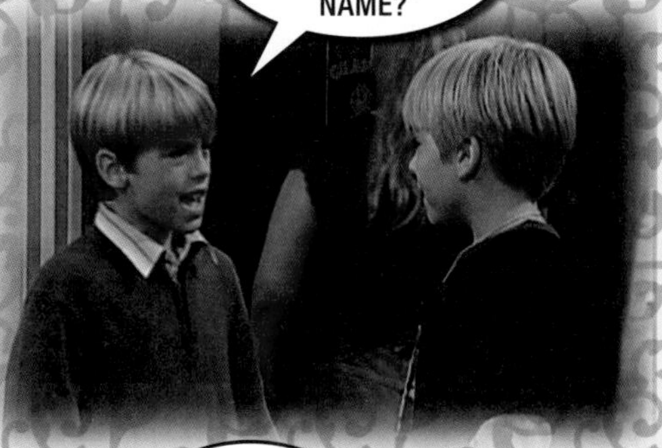
YEAH, BUT DO ANY OF THEM EVEN KNOW YOUR NAME?

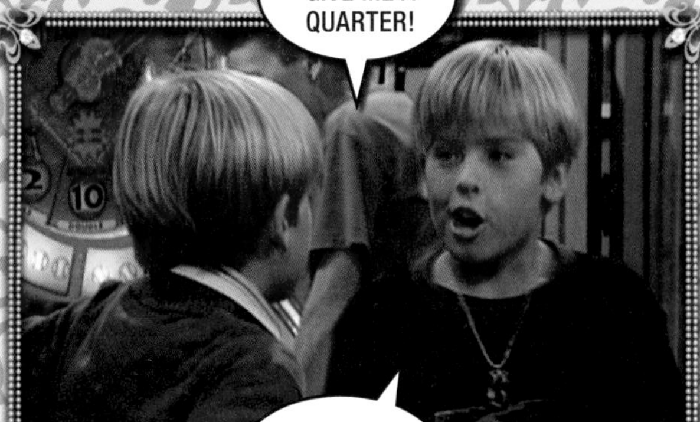
HEY, JACK. GIVE ME A QUARTER!
SEE? OFF BY ONE LETTER.

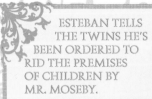

ESTEBAN TELLS THE TWINS HE'S BEEN ORDERED TO RID THE PREMISES OF CHILDREN BY MR. MOSEBY.

uh-oh

WE CAN'T ASK THEM TO LEAVE, THEY'RE OUR FRIENDS.

THEN ONE OF THE DREW CREW CALLS ZACK "ZEEK."

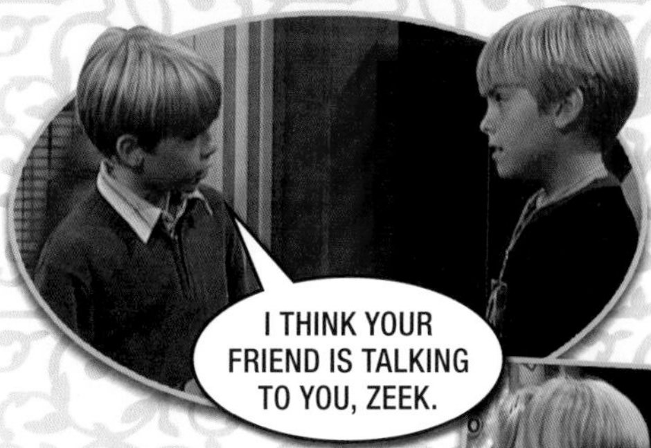
I THINK YOUR FRIEND IS TALKING TO YOU, ZEEK.

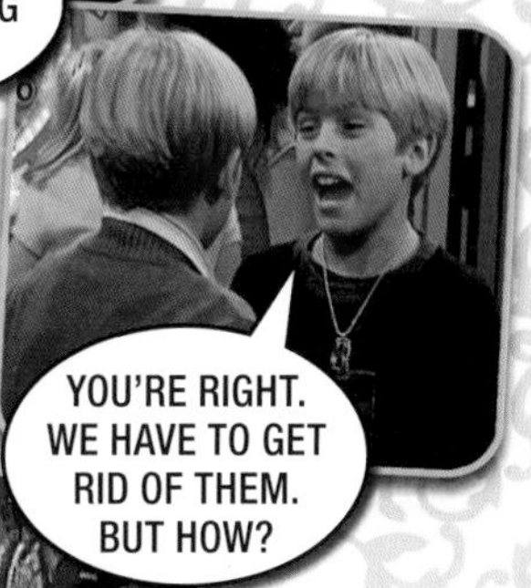
YOU'RE RIGHT. WE HAVE TO GET RID OF THEM. BUT HOW?

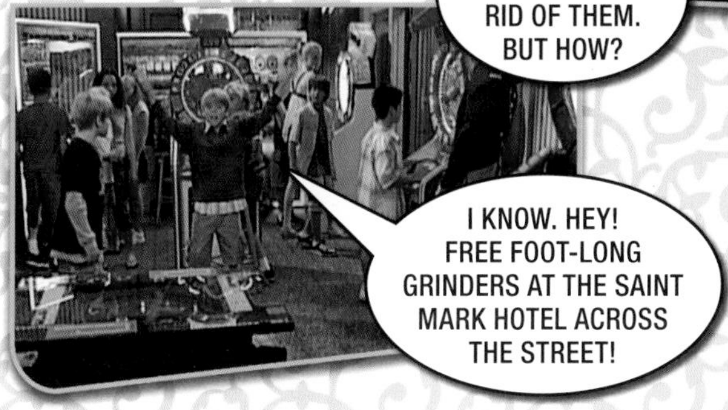
I KNOW. HEY! FREE FOOT-LONG GRINDERS AT THE SAINT MARK HOTEL ACROSS THE STREET!

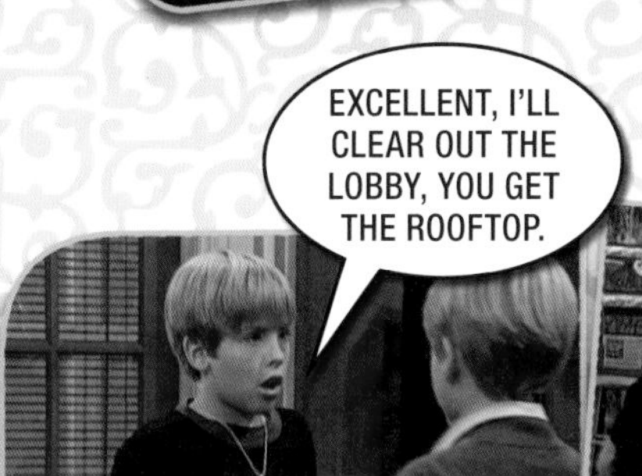
EXCELLENT, I'LL CLEAR OUT THE LOBBY, YOU GET THE ROOFTOP.

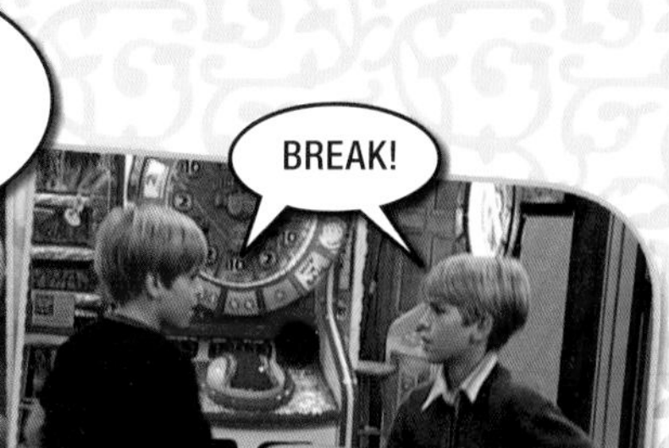
BREAK!

AT THE CANDY COUNTER, LANCE ASKS MADDIE OUT ON ANOTHER DATE. HE SUGGESTS THEY TAKE A QUICK SWIM, HIT THE JACUZZI, AND THEN WATCH THE MOVIE "SEABISCUIT."

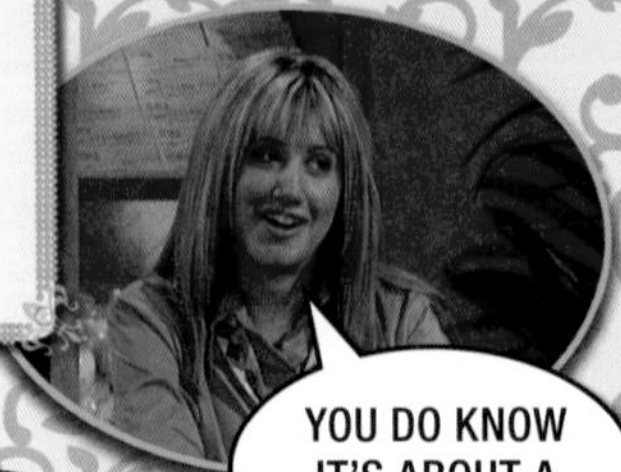
YOU DO KNOW IT'S ABOUT A HORSE.

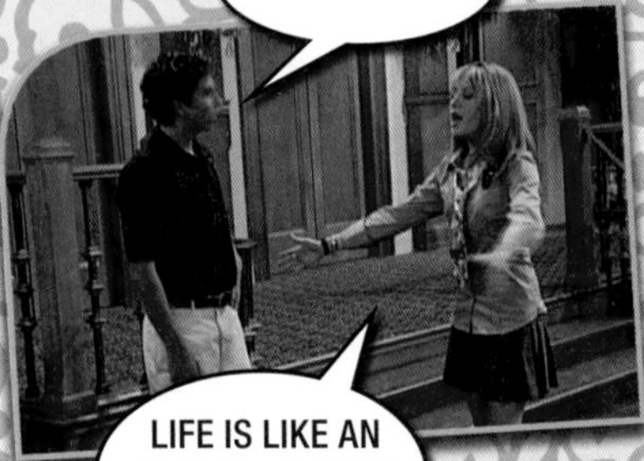
A SEAHORSE?
LIFE IS LIKE AN OCEAN—IT EBBS AND FLOWS—

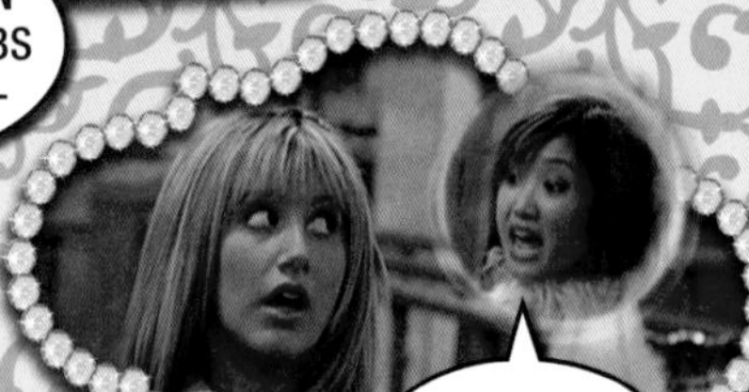
DUMP HIM NOW!

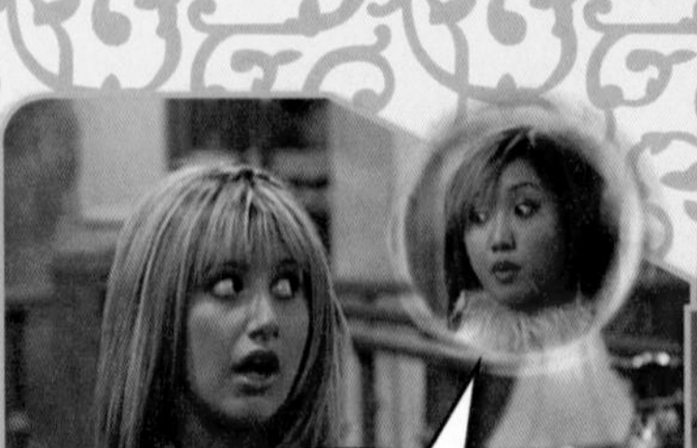
DON'T MAKE ME COME OUT OF THIS BUBBLE!

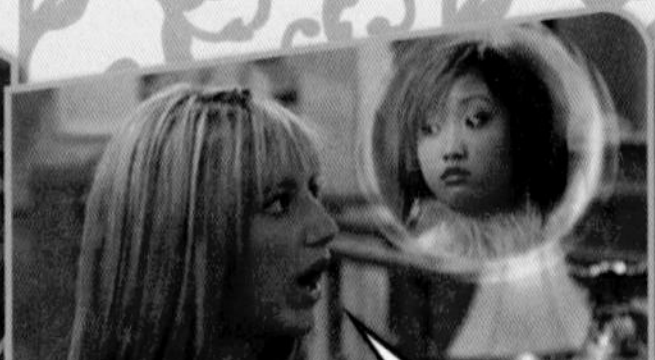
WOULD YOU BE QUIET?

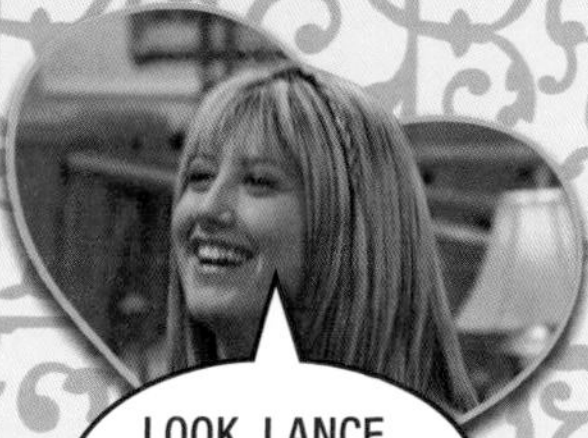
LOOK, LANCE...
LIFE IS LIKE A
RIVER—

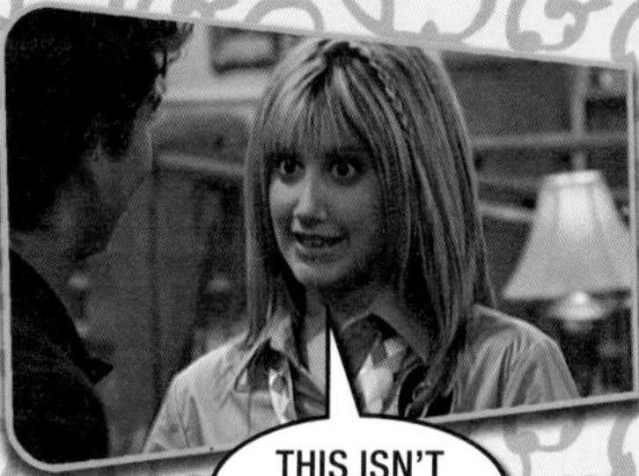
THIS ISN'T
WORKING.

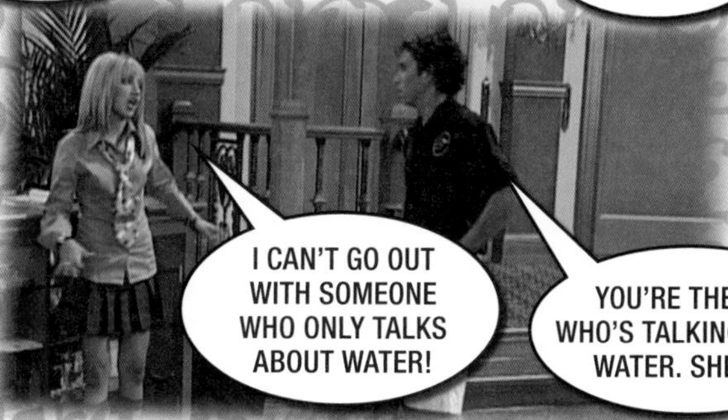
I CAN'T GO OUT
WITH SOMEONE
WHO ONLY TALKS
ABOUT WATER!
YOU'RE THE ONE
WHO'S TALKING ABOUT
WATER. SHEESH.

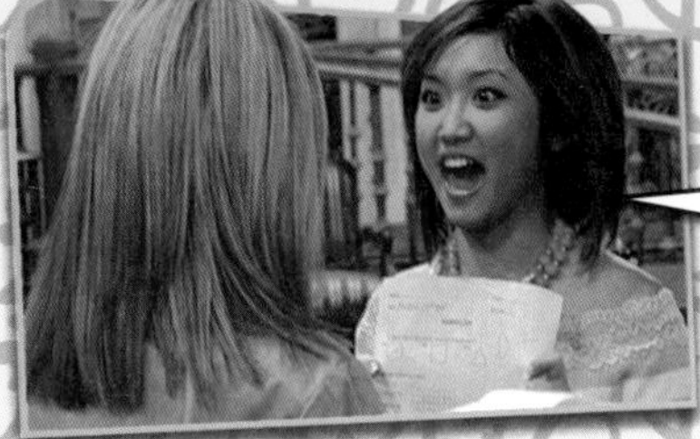
GOOD NEWS!
I GOT A D-PLUS
IN MATH!

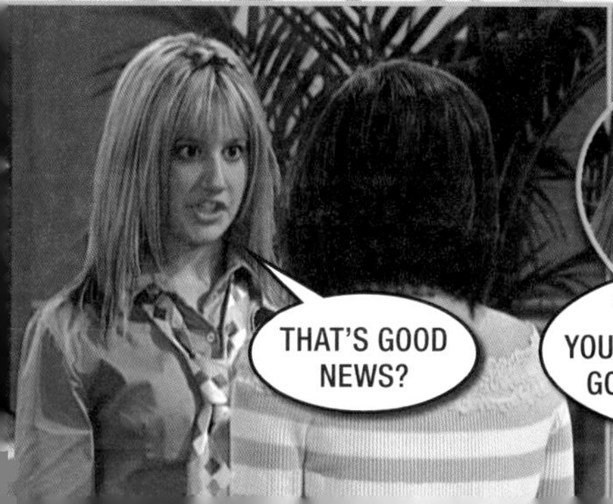
THAT'S GOOD
NEWS?

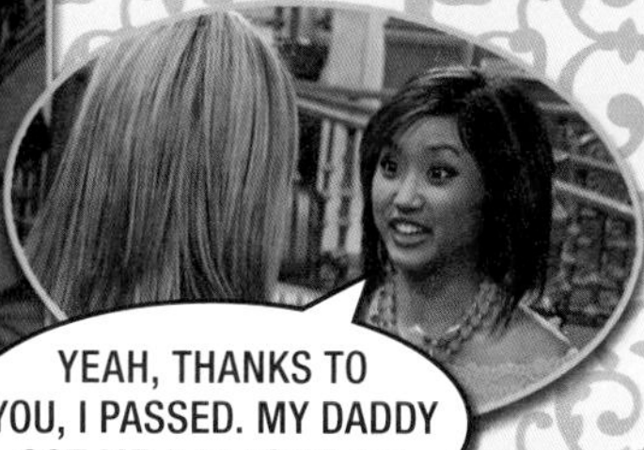
YEAH, THANKS TO
YOU, I PASSED. MY DADDY
GOT ME A PLASMA TV!

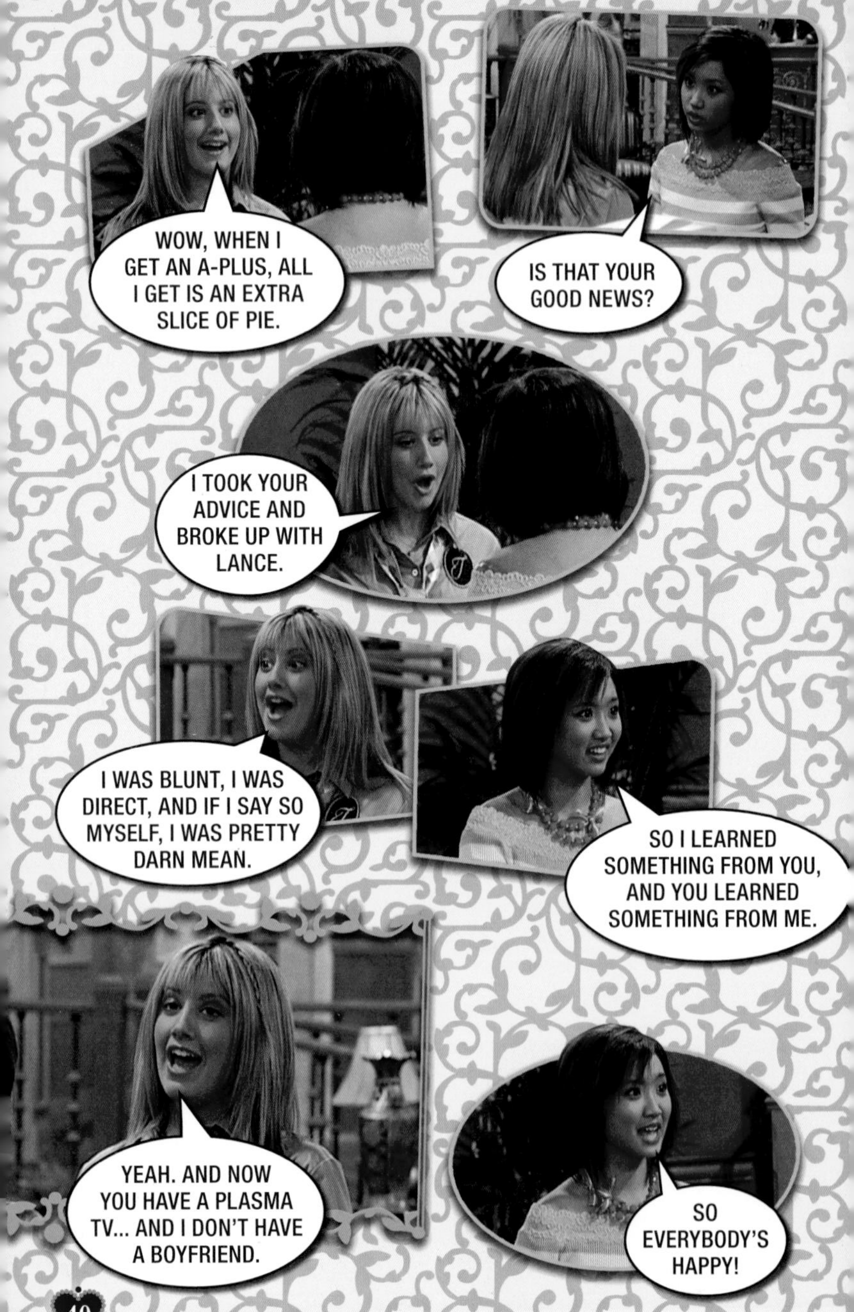
WOW, WHEN I GET AN A-PLUS, ALL I GET IS AN EXTRA SLICE OF PIE.
IS THAT YOUR GOOD NEWS?
I TOOK YOUR ADVICE AND BROKE UP WITH LANCE.
I WAS BLUNT, I WAS DIRECT, AND IF I SAY SO MYSELF, I WAS PRETTY DARN MEAN.
SO I LEARNED SOMETHING FROM YOU, AND YOU LEARNED SOMETHING FROM ME.
YEAH. AND NOW YOU HAVE A PLASMA TV... AND I DON'T HAVE A BOYFRIEND.
SO EVERYBODY'S HAPPY!

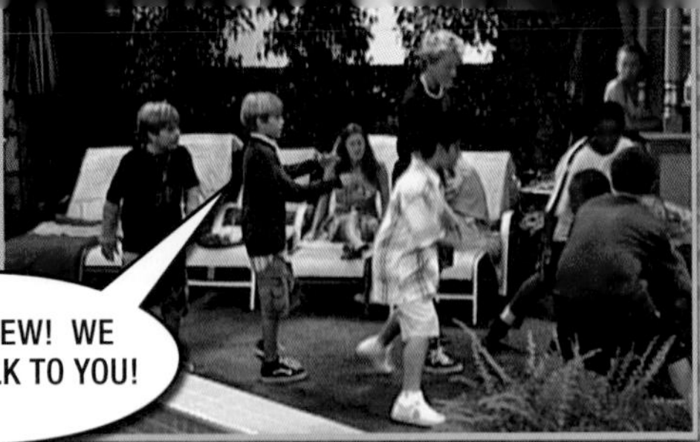
DREW! DREW! WE NEED TO TALK TO YOU!

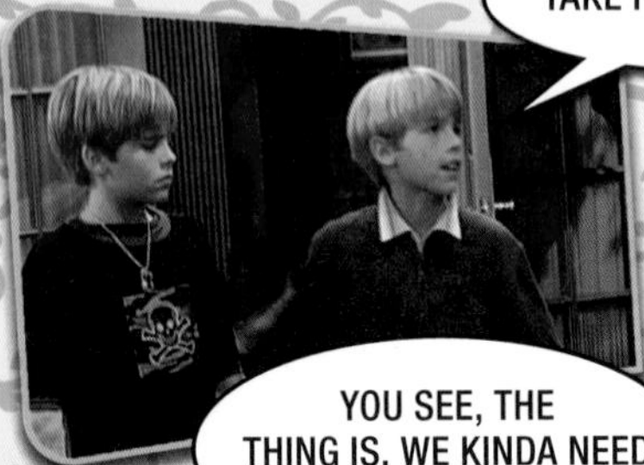
TAKE IT AWAY, ZACK.

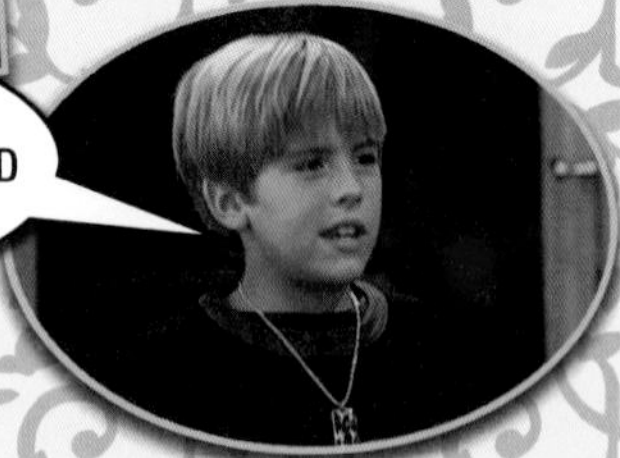
YOU SEE, THE THING IS, WE KINDA NEED YA TO LEAVE.

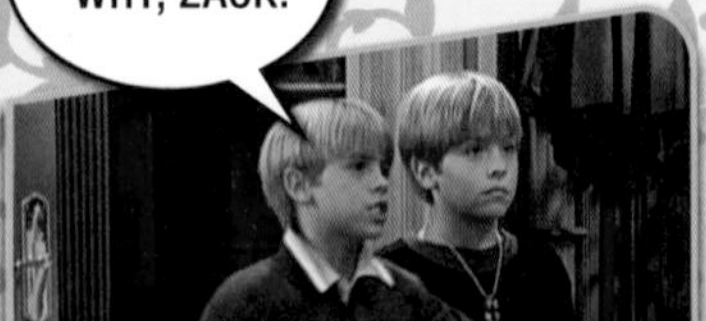
TELL HIM WHY, ZACK.

DREW SAYS IF HE AND HIS FRIENDS LEAVE, THEY'RE NOT COMING BACK...SO THE TWINS WILL HAVE TO HANG WITH THOSE "DWEEBS," MAX AND SILKWORM.

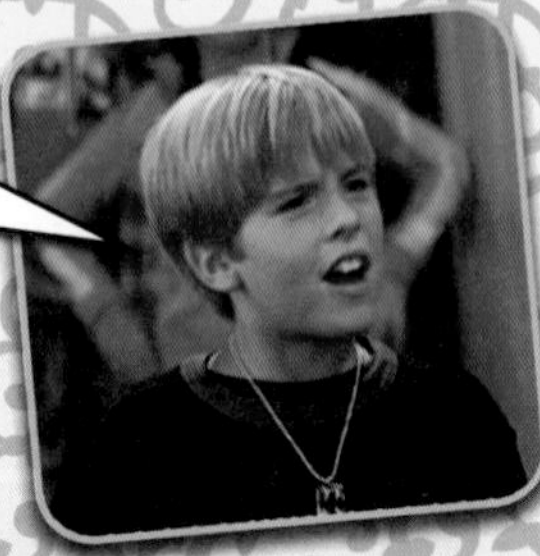
HIS NAME IS TAPEWORM. AND HE'S OUR FRIEND. AND SO IS THE OTHER DWEEB.

46

47

LATER, AT THE ROOFTOP POOL...

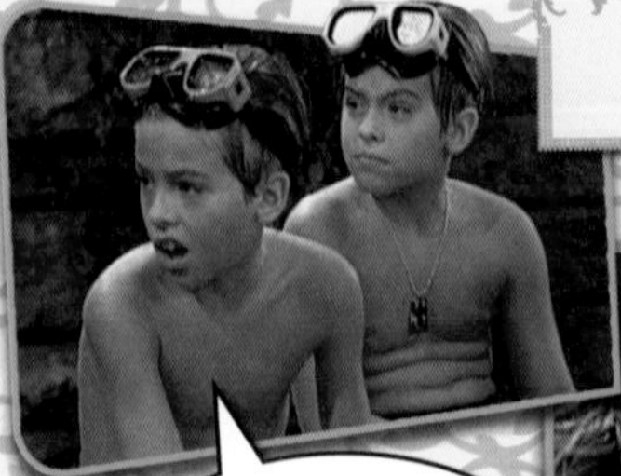
THIS IS THE WORST PUNISHMENT WE EVER GOT.

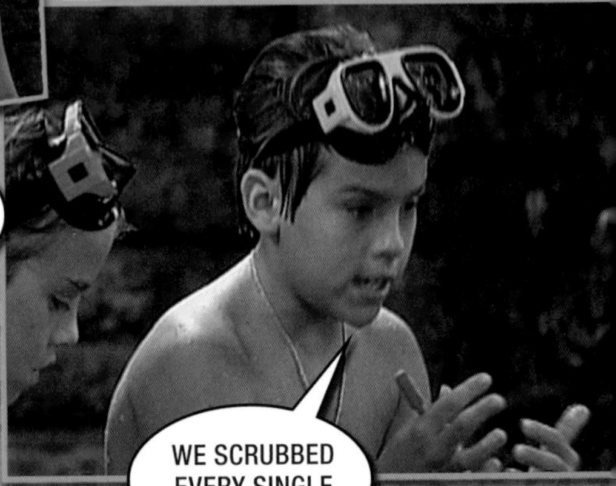
WE SCRUBBED EVERY SINGLE TILE.

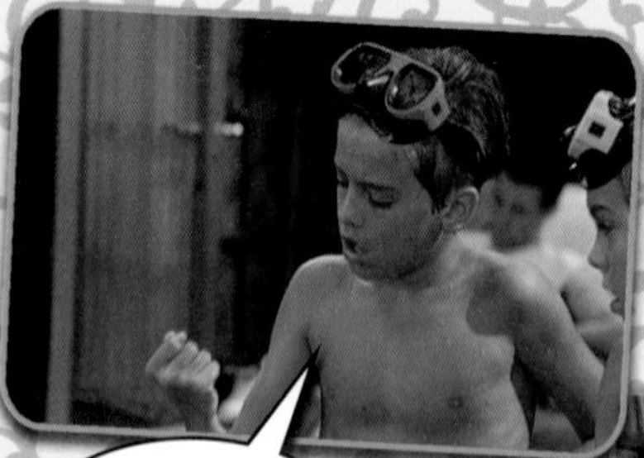
I CAN'T UNCURL MY FINGERS.

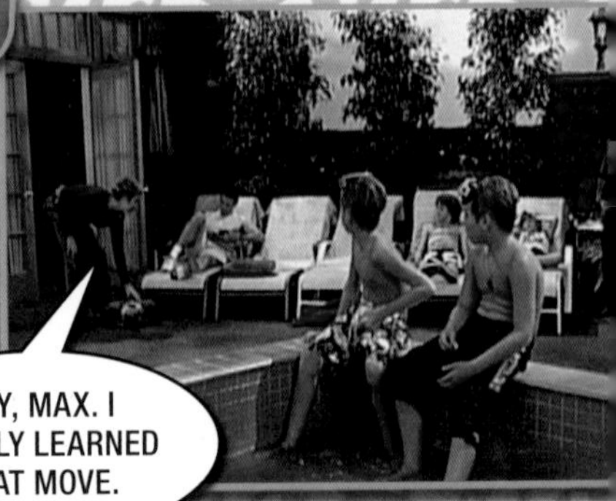
HEY, MAX. I FINALLY LEARNED THAT MOVE.

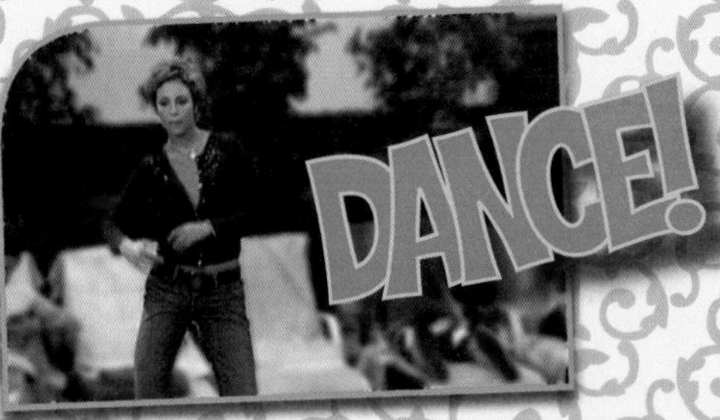
DANCE!

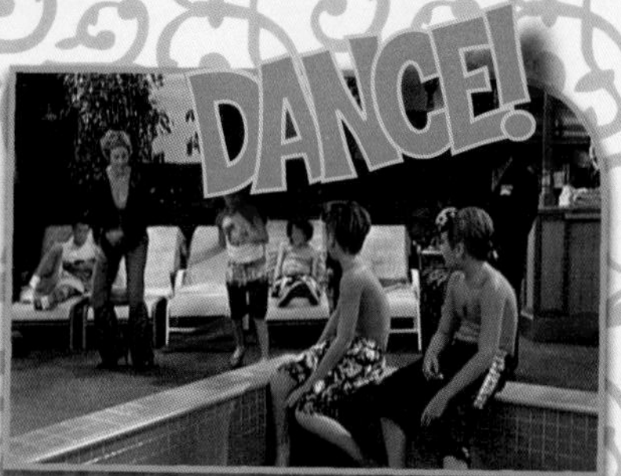
DANCE!

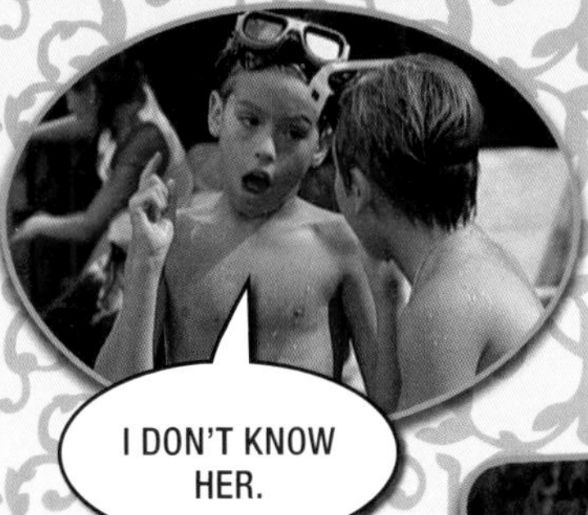
I DON'T KNOW HER.

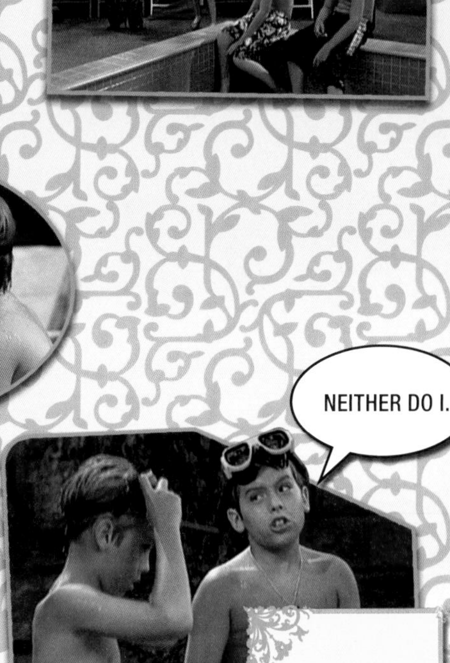
NEITHER DO I.
THE END

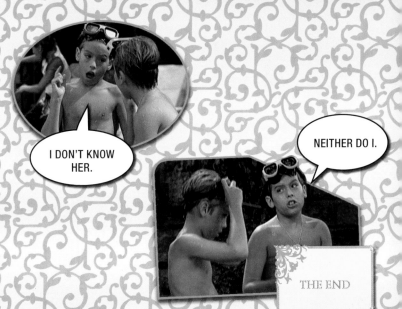

Disney

The Suite Life of Zack & Cody

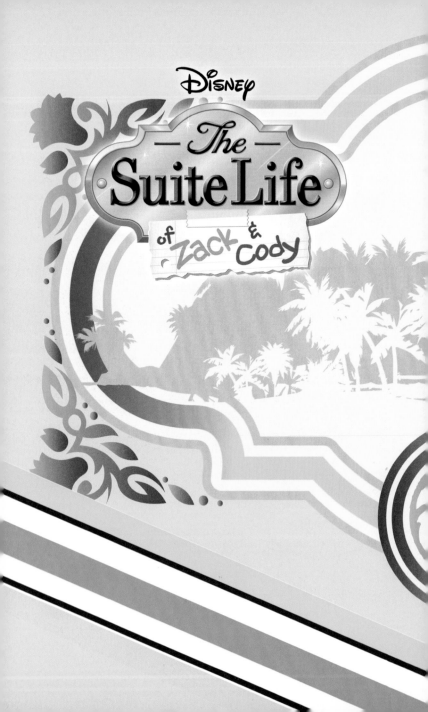

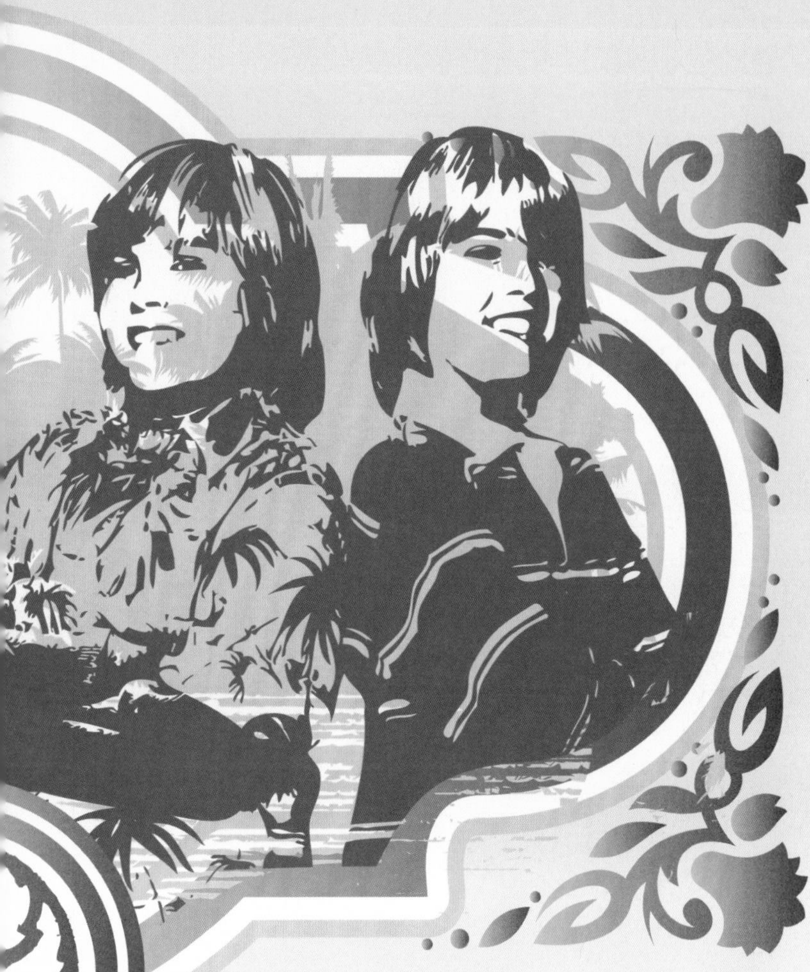

MADDIE CHECKS IN

BASED ON THE EPISODE
WRITTEN BY DANNY KALLIS & JIM GEOGHAN

MADDIE COMES IN...

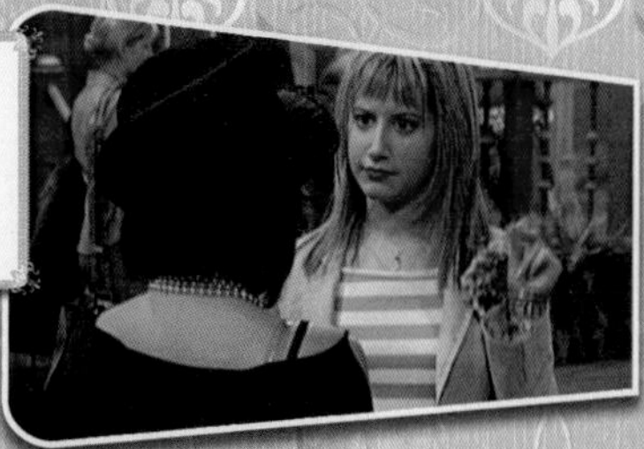

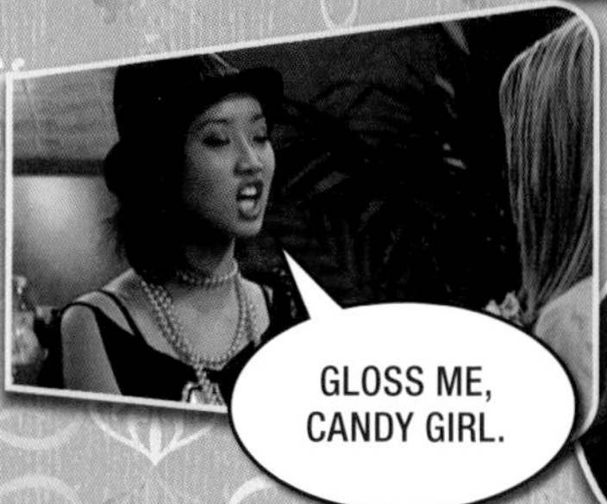
GLOSS ME, CANDY GIRL.

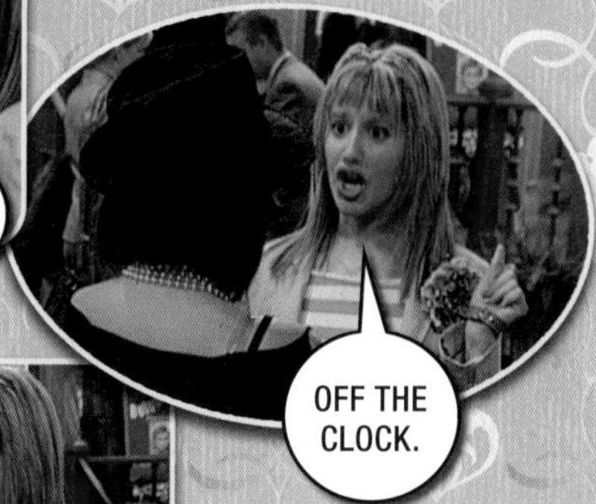
OFF THE CLOCK.

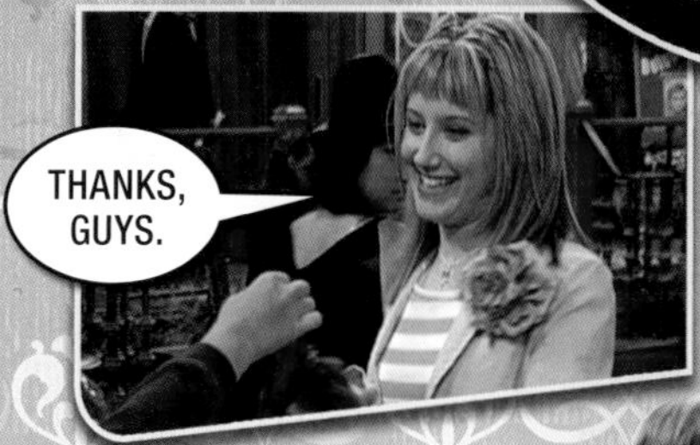
THANKS, GUYS.

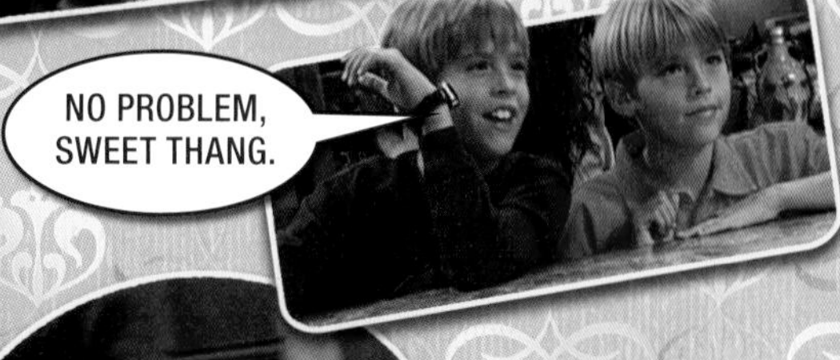
NO PROBLEM, SWEET THANG.

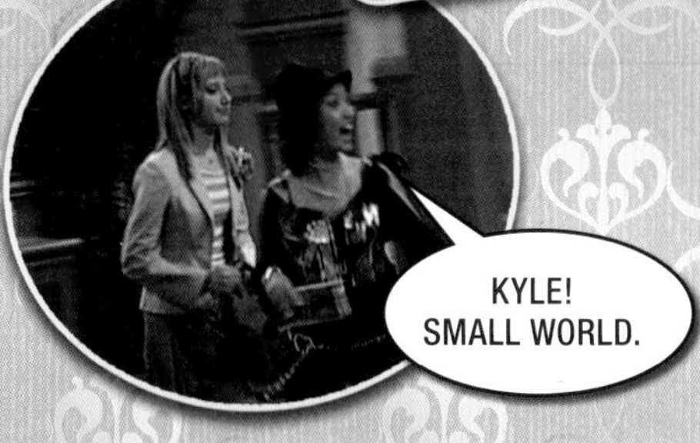
KYLE! SMALL WORLD.

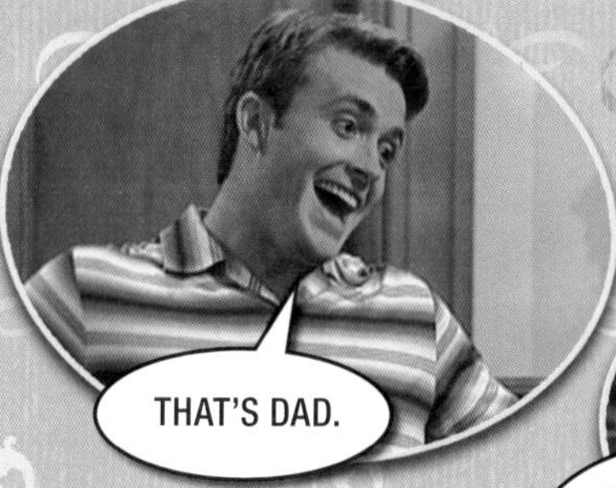
THAT'S DAD.
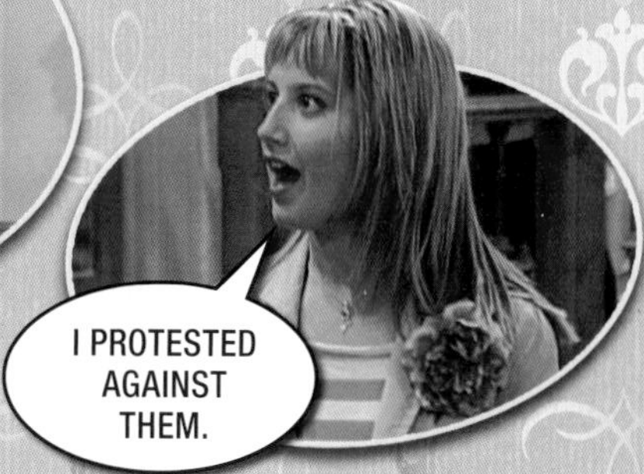
I PROTESTED AGAINST THEM.
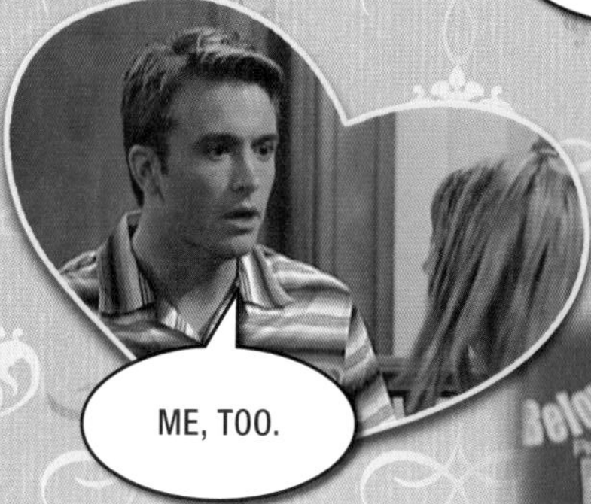
ME, TOO.
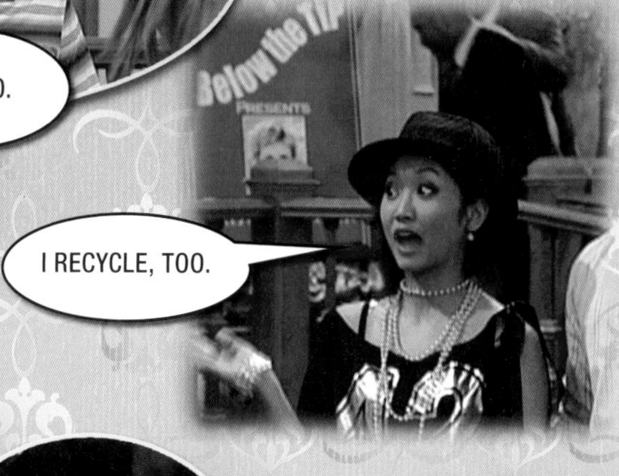
I RECYCLE, TOO.
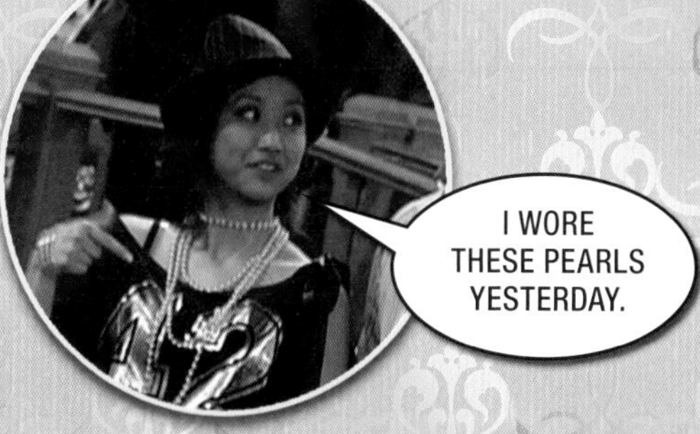
I WORE THESE PEARLS YESTERDAY.

KYLE TELLS LONDON THAT MADDIE IS ALL JASON COULD TALK ABOUT LAST NIGHT... AND THAT JASON THINKS MADDIE IS RICH.

WHAT? HE THOUGHT— HA! I DON'T WANT TO BURST ANY BUBBLES... BUT IT'S SO MUCH FUN!

LONDON, A WORD.

I COULDN'T HELP OVERHEARING YOUR PLANS—

63

67

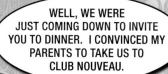

WELL, WE WERE JUST COMING DOWN TO INVITE YOU TO DINNER. I CONVINCED MY PARENTS TO TAKE US TO CLUB NOUVEAU.

REALLY? WOW... I CAN'T GO. YEAH, I PROMISED I'D BABYSIT THE BOYS TONIGHT.

CODY, HEY, JOSH CALLED. WE'RE SLEEPING OVER AT HIS HOUSE TONIGHT.

JASON'S DAD INSISTS THAT MADDIE JOIN THEM. HE TELLS MADDIE THEY'LL PICK HER UP AT SEVEN O'CLOCK SHARP.

WHEN MADDIE TELLS THE TWINS SHE DOESN'T HAVE ANYTHING TO WEAR TO CLUB NOUVEAU, THEY ACCEPT THE CHALLENGE.

HEY, ESTEBAN! MOSEBY'S YELLING FOR YOU.

WELL, YOU'RE KEEPING A GREAT MAN WAITING.

BUT THIS DRESS MUST GO TO LONDON.

WE'LL TAKE IT.

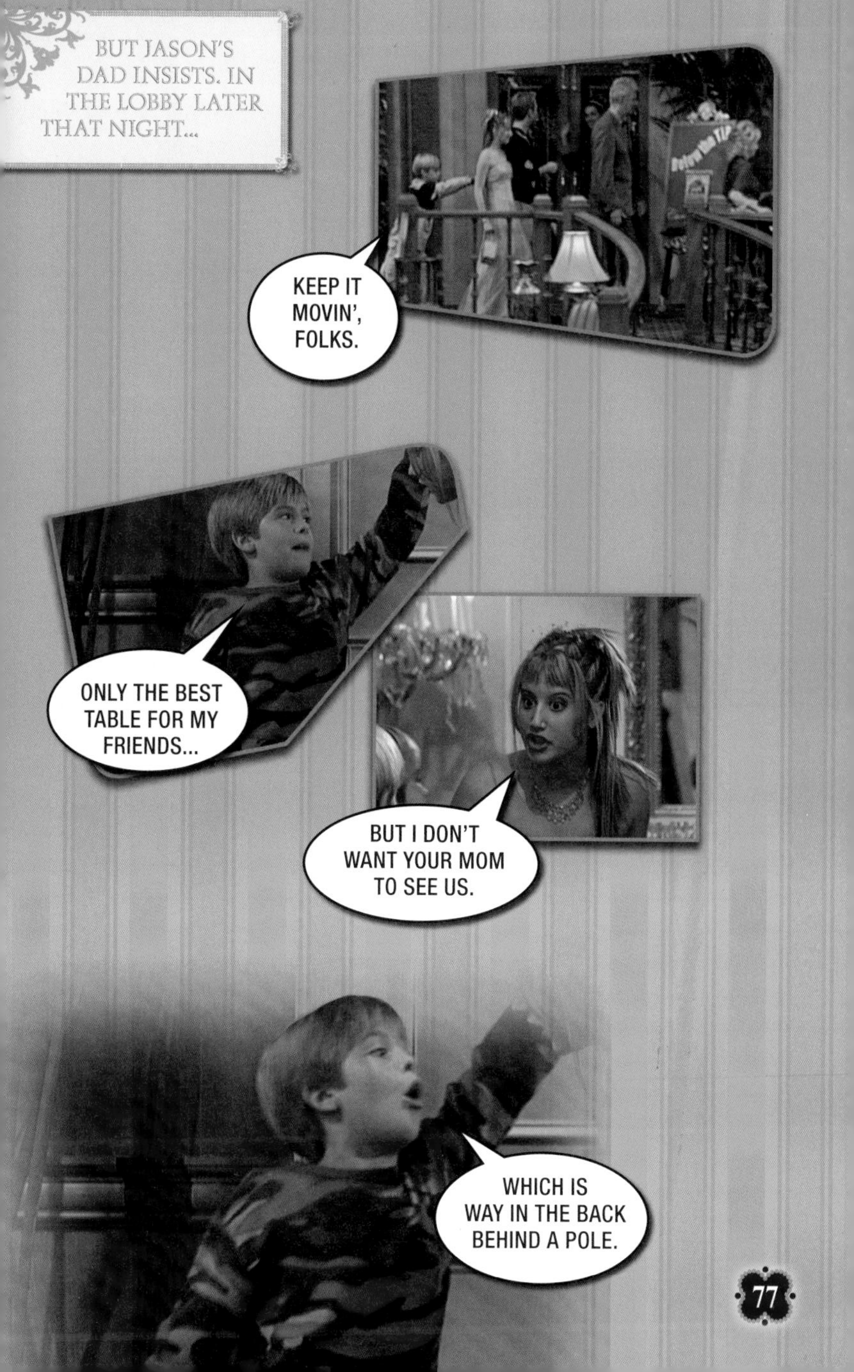
BUT JASON'S DAD INSISTS. IN THE LOBBY LATER THAT NIGHT...
KEEP IT MOVIN', FOLKS.
ONLY THE BEST TABLE FOR MY FRIENDS...
BUT I DON'T WANT YOUR MOM TO SEE US.
WHICH IS WAY IN THE BACK BEHIND A POLE.

EXCUSE ME, MR. AMPUTATOR. COULD I HAVE YOUR AUTOGRAPH?

WELL, OF COURSE YOU CAN, YOUNG MAN.

COULD YOU WRITE, "TO CODY... A YOUNG MAN I HAVE JUST MET— MET IS M-E-T...

"AND YET, I FEEL AS IF I'VE KNOWN FOR A LONG, LONG, LONG..."

OH, IS THERE NO END TO THIS NOVEL?! MY APOLOGIES.

DON'T WORRY. I PUT "TO, CODY. LOVE, THE AMPUTATOR." HOW'S THAT?

YEAH, THAT'S COOL.

79

82

QUICK!

DROP!

DASH!

000, A QUARTER.

BEND

ZACK CLOSES THE DOOR BEFORE AMPUTATOR SEES HIM...

84

85

TOKYOPOP
Disney
Hannah Montana
CINE-MANGA
TOKYOPOP
Disney
CINE-MANGA
Hannah Montana
SECRETS AND SUPERSNEAKS
AVAILABLE NOW AT TOKYOPOP
© Disney Enterprises, Inc.